THE
HOLLYWOOD
VEGETARIAN
COOKBOOK

THE HOLLYWOOD

VEGETARIAN

COOKBOOK

Lean, Healthy Meals From America's Celebrity Kitchens

Francia Ruppen

A Birch Lane Press Book
Published by Carol Publishing Group

Designed by Stephanie Tevonian Design

A Birch Lane Press Book
Published by Carol Publishing Group
Birch Lane Press is a registered trademark of Carol Communications, Inc.
Editorial Offices: 600 Madison Avenue, New York, N.Y. 10022
Sales and Distribution Offices: 120 Enterprise Avenue, Secaucus, N.J. 07094
In Canada: Canadian Manda Group, One Atlantic Avenue, Suite 105, Toronto, Ontario M6K 3E7
Queries regarding rights and permissions should be addressed to Carol Publishing Group, 600 Madison Avenue, New York, N.Y. 10022

Carol Publishing Group books are available at special discounts for bulk purchases, sales promotion, fund-raising, or educational purposes. Special editions can be created to specifications. For details, contact: Special Sales Department, Carol Publishing Group, 120 Enterprise Avenue, Secaucus, N.J. 07094

Manufactured in the United States of America
10 9 8 7 6 5 4 3 2 1

Library of Congress Cataloging-in-Publication Data
Ruppen, Francia.
    The Hollywood vegetarian cookbook : lean, healthy meals from America's celebrity kitchens / by Francia Ruppen.
        p.   cm.
    "A Birch Lane Press book."
    ISBN 1-55972-288-6
    1. Vegetarian cookery.   2. Celebrities—California—Los Angeles.   I Title.
TX837.R924   1995
641.5'636—dc20
                                                94-44285
                                                CIP

This book is dedicated to the memory of Audrey Hepburn whose tireless efforts to fight world hunger are missed.

CONTENTS

CONTENTS

CONTENTS

CONTENTS

CONTENTS

CONTENTS

A DOCTOR'S VIEW

A vegetarian diet is probably the healthiest way to eat. It's much more difficult to eat too much fat if you're eating vegetarian, and it's an excellent way to increase your intake of "good" nutrients—complex carbohydrates, vitamins and minerals, and foods that have been less processed. Processing—cooking, freezing, and other methods of preserving foods—often robs them of some of their nutrient value, especially vitamins. Meats, especially, often contain additives that may be harmful, including antibiotics used to prevent illness in animals as well as illness from food poisoning in humans that consume them. The additives themselves often cause allergic reactions and other problems for people who eat foods treated this way.

And it isn't hard to make sure you're getting enough protein by eating vegetarian, even for growing children. A few simple rules about combining vegetarian foods are all you need to remember. The foods can be easy to prepare and they are usually delicious—that's what this book is about. Many people find changing from a meat-containing diet to a vegetarian diet a lot easier than they thought it would be, and it can result in greater feelings of well-being and in lower cholesterol levels. Even if you're not considering eliminating meat altogether right now, you can have many of the benefits of vegetarianism by eating meatless meals one or more days a week.

So try a few (or all) of the recipes you find here, and enjoy!

Dr. Sarah Towne
Graduate City Avenue Hospital
Philadelphia

ACKNOWLEDGMENTS

This book is the result of input and cooperation from many people. First and foremost, wholehearted appreciation must be given to the celebrities who have magnanimously contributed their recipes and photographs for this project.

Special thanks to Patricia Gallagher for her technical guidance, and to Carol Wiley Lorente, food editor of Vegetarian Times, for her kind input.

Heartfelt thanks and particular recognition to my daughter, Kristina, for countless hours of work on the nutritional analyses, and to my husband, Andrew, for his eternal, unwavering patience and support.

A generous portion of the proceeds of this book are being donated in support of animal rights and to OXFAM to help alleviate world hunger.

INTRODUCTION

If you don't own a vegetarian cookbook, this one is an interesting, user-friendly place to start. The panoply of recipes—some familiar, some exotic—provides a diverse sampling to tempt, nourish, and satisfy. Each recipe includes a handy nutritional breakdown that provides the au fait *macronutrient profile of the dish.*

In addition, I have provided a streamlined or "REDUX" version of many of the recipes. Sodium, fat, and cholesterol are targets for reductions; calories usually drop as well. Care is taken to maintain the taste and integrity of the dish. The REDUX recipes are a metagenesis of the originals for all who are concerned about the balance of nutrients in their diet. REDUX recipes are a way to reshape the nutritional profile of a favorite and can be a real timesaver for those interested in eating lighter. These REDUX versions can be found in Part Two.

If you are familiar with other vegetarian cookbooks, you'll soon discover that this is more than just another source of great recipes to augment your repetoire. This is cooking and living for the next millennium, when robust good health will be a coveted asset.

Eating more vegetarian meals, curtailing intake of meat and dairy is a terrific beginning to eating healthy. If you ever needed incentive for starting to eat a little healthier and taking a little better care of yourself—and your world, this book is it. Use it and enjoy!

KEY

☆ Low-fat version provided in Celebrity Redux, beginning on page 131.

* Brand name used for purposes of the Nutritional Analysis following recipe; not specified in original version.

RECIPE V-SCALE

The following is a list indicating where each recipe fits on the Vegetarian or "V-Scale." If you follow a particular vegetarian diet, you might want to consult this list.

ANIMAL	Marshmallow Sweet Potatoes
ANIMAL-LACTO	Cottage Cheese Salad
ANIMAL-LACTO-OVO	Cassis Caviar
ANIMAL-OVO	Caesar Salad
LACTO	Tim's Favorite Manly Man Lasagne
	Greek Pasta Salad
	Vegetable Medley
	Vegetable Casserole
	Saffron Risotto With Arugula and Wild Mushrooms
	Chevy and Jayni's Vegetable Lasagne
	Vegetable Cottage Pie
	Grilled Veggies
	Sicilian Cheese Casserole
	Parmesan Eggplant Casserole
	Steamed Veggies
	Potatoes Lynda
	Givetch
	Fettucine Alfredo
	Nutty Cheese Roll
	Beetroot Cream Soup
	Vegetable Pie

RECIPE V-SCALE

Pasta With Fresh Tomatoes
Pasta With Tomato Sauce
O'Redgrave's Irish Soda Bread
Baked Rice
Pasta With Pesto Sauce and Broccoli

LACTO-OVO

Broccoli's Farfel Stuffing
Carrot-Zucchini Muffins
Aunt Carol's Banana Wanana Nutty Wuddy Bread
Stuffed and Rolled Eggplant Marinara
Herbed Zucchini Latkes With Roasted Peppers
Dot's Bread Pudding
Sugar Cookies
Hot Artichoke Dip
Spinach Dip
Bob's Favorite Lemon Pie
Corn Pudding
Thomas Jefferson's Chess Pie
Tofu Burgers
Gin Fizz Egg Pie
Walnut Trifle
Hilda's Caramel Custard

OVO

Fat-Free Oat Bran Muffins

VEGAN

Nut Loaf
Cajun Red Beans and Rice
Soup Francine
Tabouli My Way

Amy and Desi's Pasta Delight
Balsamic Roasted New Potatoes
Mango–Black Bean Sauce Over Rice
Hot 'n' Spicy Okra
Marge and Daniel's Red Lentil Soup
Roasted Brussels Sprouts
Stuffed Nutted Squash
Chicory and Kidney Bean Salad
Christmas Pickles
My Brother's Salsa
Indonesian Salad With Spicy Peanut Dressing
Minestrone
Eggplant Sauce with Pasta
Ratatouille
Estelle's Baked Beans
Eggplant Rodriguez
Green Banana Salad
Vegetable Health Soup
Low-Cal Vinaigrette
Joan's Hummus
Roasted Eggplant Soup
Dennis and Gerry's Vegetable Soup

THE SKINNY ON FAT

Yes! You really can lose weight and keep it off—but if you think you can just diet to do it, your chances of success are about the only thing destined to be slim. If you have had problems finding a program you can live with, maybe you need a new approach. Here are a few ideas to help you along:

- *You can't look and feel perfect by "dieting" throughout your lifetime. If you set out with a "diet mentality"—trying to lose weight to reach a "goal weight"—you will end up disappointed and unhealthy. The focus belongs on nutrition and health, not on weight loss. Diets fail because they are temporary, usually highly regimented programs that are abandoned once the goal is achieved—or before.*
- *The only way to look and feel vibrantly beautiful inside and out is to be in good health—the keys to which are sensible nutrition and moderate exercise. You won't be healthy and gorgeous subsisting on sugary or processed foods. Instead, eat fresh, raw foods in small meals throughout the day, and eat "lower on the food chain."*
- *The healthiest, most sustaining diet is low in calories and fat and is nutritionally balanced. Read the labels on foods to determine their fat content. Quick tip: The number of fat grams multiplied by 10, and divided by the number of total calories gives a fast estimate of the percentage of fat in the food. Example: 2 grams of fat, 100 calories is equal to 20 (2 X 10) divided by 100: or about 20 percent fat.*
- *The American Heart Association recommends that your total fat intake not exceed 30 percent of your diet. An easy way to achieve this is to stay away from individual foods that are over 30 percent fat. Simple!*
- *Metabolism-fitness. A conscientiously applied workout regimen will increase*

your metabolism so that you burn fat faster. Something as simple as a twenty-minute walk three times a week can up your metabolic rate. Remember to check with your doctor before starting any new exercise program.

• *Sugar and fat are best friends—where sugar is, fat will accumulate. Sugar knocks out chromium, which metabolizes fat. So even if a food is low in fat, if it's high in sugar, it promotes fat and is no friend of yours.*

FOOD GUIDE PYRAMID
A Guide to Daily Food Choices

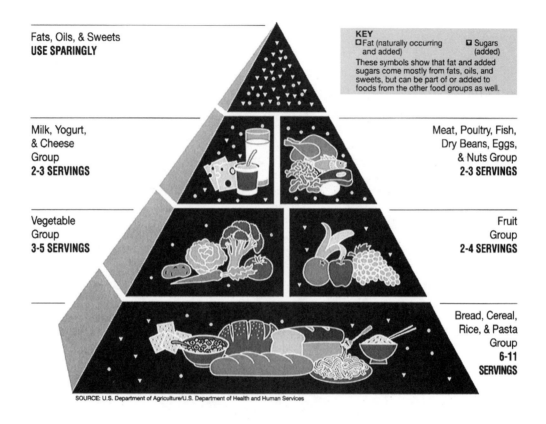

Fats, Oils, & Sweets
USE SPARINGLY

KEY
□ Fat (naturally occurring and added) ▨ Sugars (added)
These symbols show that fat and added sugars come mostly from fats, oils, and sweets, but can be part of or added to foods from the other food groups as well.

Milk, Yogurt, & Cheese Group
2-3 SERVINGS

Meat, Poultry, Fish, Dry Beans, Eggs, & Nuts Group
2-3 SERVINGS

Vegetable Group
3-5 SERVINGS

Fruit Group
2-4 SERVINGS

Bread, Cereal, Rice, & Pasta Group
6-11 SERVINGS

SOURCE: U.S. Department of Agriculture/U.S. Department of Health and Human Services

A Closer Look at Fat and Added Sugars

The small tip of the Pyramid shows fats, oils, and sweets. These are foods such as salad dressings, cream, butter, margarine, sugars, soft drinks, candies,  and sweet desserts. Alcoholic beverages are also part of this group. These foods provide calories but few vitamins and minerals. Most people should go easy on foods from this group.

 Some fat or sugar symbols are shown in the other food groups. That's to remind you that some foods in these groups can also be high in fat and added sugars, such as cheese or ice cream from the milk group, or french fries from the vegetable group. When choosing foods for a healthful diet, consider the fat and added sugars in your choices from all the food groups, not just fats, oils, and sweets from the Pyramid tip.

PART 1

CELEBRITIES

AND THEIR RECIPES

GRANT ALEKSANDER

GRANT ALEKSANDER

☆ Nut Loaf

6 Servings

1 teaspoon vegetable oil

½ cup raw wheat germ

1½ cups cooked long-grain brown rice

¾ cup walnuts, chopped

¼ cup sunflower seeds

1 large onion, chopped

8 ounces Soya Kaas* soy Cheddar cheese

½ teaspoon salt

½ teaspoon black pepper

4 Ener-G* egg substitutes

8 ounces Health Valley* tomato sauce

Preheat oven to 350°F. Oil a 9-inch loaf pan. Combine all remaining ingredients (except tomato sauce) and pack into oiled pan. Bake 50 minutes. Cool 10 minutes. Serve with tomato sauce.

Nutritional Analysis   *for 1 serving {206 g}*

Calories 350   Calories from fat 188

Nutrient:	% Calories from:	Nutrient:	% Calories from:
Total fat 21 g	52 %	Total carbohydrate 27 g	30 %
Saturated fat 2 g	6 %	Dietary fiber 3 g	
Cholesterol 0 mg		Sugars 2 g	
Sodium 556 mg		Protein 17 g	19 %

% Daily:

Vitamin A, 4 %; Vitamin C, 12 %; Calcium, 3 %; Iron, 11 %

STEVE ALLEN AND JANE MEADOWS

Cajun Red Beans and Rice

4 Servings

*1 serving cooking spray
(a 1-second spray)*

1 cup onions, chopped/fine

*2 garlic cloves, peeled and
minced*

1 bell pepper, chopped

1 cup sliced celery

*1 15-ounce can kidney or red
beans, rinsed and drained*

*8 ounces Pritikin Original
Spaghetti Sauce*

1 teaspoon dried thyme

¾ teaspoon Tabasco sauce

3 cups hot, cooked brown rice

Lightly spray a 10-inch skillet with cooking spray.
Add onion and garlic and cook 3 minutes, or until
tender, stirring frequently. Add pepper, celery,
beans, sauce, and spices. Simmer on low heat for 15
minutes or until veggies are all crisp-tender. Serve
over rice.

Nutritional Analysis   *for 1 serving {425 g}*

Calories 544   Calories from fat 29

Nutrient: % Calories from:	Nutrient: % Calories from:
Total fat 3 g 5 %	Total carbohydrate 105 g 75 %
Saturated fat 0 g 1 %	Dietary fiber 10 g
Cholesterol 0 mg	Sugars 3 g
Sodium 62 mg	Protein 28 g 20 %

% Daily:

Vitamin A, 2 %; Vitamin C, 68 %; Calcium, 12 %; Iron, 49 %

TIM ALLEN

TIM ALLEN

☆ Tim's Favorite Manly Man Lasagne

8 Servings

1 pound eggplant

½ teaspoon salt

2 garlic cloves

1 large onion

1 bell pepper

1½ pounds carrots

1½ pounds leeks, well rinsed

2 teaspoons butter

2 tablespoons olive oil

2 pounds ricotta cheese

2 teaspoons salt

¼ teaspoon black pepper

30 ounces Health Valley* tomato sauce

½ pound lasagne, uncooked weight, boiled until not quite done (it will finish while the dish bakes)

½ pound mozzarella cheese, sliced thin

⅓ cup grated Parmesan cheese

Peel and chop eggplant; sprinkle lightly with salt and allow to "sweat" for about 20 minutes. Preheat oven to 400°F. Peel and mince garlic. Chop onion, bell pepper, carrots, and leeks. Butter a large, rectangular baking dish or lasagne pan. Sauté chopped onion in olive oil for about 10 minutes until transparent, but not brown. Add minced garlic and the vegetables. Cover and sauté until tender, about 15 minutes. Mix in ricotta, salt, and pepper. Cover the bottom of the baking dish with a layer of tomato sauce. Cover with a layer of lasagne, followed by a layer of the vegetable mixture. Cover this with a layer of mozzarella slices. Repeat until all ingredients are used, finishing with a layer of sauce. Sprinkle any remaining mozzarella and the Parmesean cheese on top. Bake 1 hour. If the lasagne is getting too brown toward the end of the time, cover the dish. Allow to set up before cutting. *Variation:* Replace eggplant with zucchini.

Nutritional Analysis   *for 1 serving {566g}*
Calories 601   Calories from fat 257

Nutrient: % Calories from:	Nutrient: % Calories from:
Total fat 29 g 42 %	Total carbohydrate 59 g 39 %
Saturated fat 15 g 22 %	Dietary fiber 5 g
Cholesterol 88 mg	Sugars 13 g
Sodium 1034 mg	Protein 29 g 19 %

% Daily:
Vitamin A, 275 %; Vitamin C, 84 %; Calcium, 56 %; Iron, 28 %

RICHARD ANDERSON

RICHARD ANDERSON
☆ Greek Pasta Salad

6 Servings

2½ pounds plum tomatoes

8 ounces Sargento* feta cheese

2 tablespoons fresh basil leaves, chopped

4 garlic cloves, peeled and minced

25 Greek olives, pitted

¼ cup olive oil

1 teaspoon balsamic vinegar

1 pound penne or similar pasta

Wash and core tomatoes, cutting off stems and removing seeds (a grapefruit knife is handy for this procedure). Dice tomatoes and put into a large mixing bowl with crumbled feta, basil, garlic, olives, and olive oil, mixing gently but thoroughly. When each ingredient is coated with olive oil, splash on the balsamic vinegar. Allow to develop at room temperature for about 20–30 minutes. Meanwhile, cook the pasta in boiling water, drain, and put back into dry cooking pot immediately. Toss the fresh sauce in with steaming pasta; cover, let stand for 3–5 minutes. "Delicious served with warm, fresh French bread or rolls. Serve and Enjoy!!!"

Nutritional Analysis *for 1 serving {454 g}*

Calories 966   Calories from fat 533

Nutrient:	% Calories from:	Nutrient:	% Calories from:
Total fat 59 g	53 %	Total carbohydrate 73 g	29 %
Saturated fat 24 g	22 %	Dietary fiber 4 g	
Cholesterol 121 mg		Sugars 6 g	
Sodium 2,697 mg		Protein 44 g	18 %

% Daily:

Vitamin A, 37 %; Vitamin C, 62 %; Calcium, 87 %; Iron, 26 %

JULIE ANDREWS

JULIE ANDREWS
Soup Francine

2 Servings

1 large onion, to make 1 cup, diced

1 medium potato

1 tablespoon Heart Beat* canola oil

2 carrots

2 cups diced celery

8 ounces broccoli

¾ cup Health Valley* frozen peas

½ teaspoon black pepper

1 teaspoon salt

¼ cup fresh parsley

½ teaspoon curry powder

2 teaspoons fines herbes (mixed herbs)

2 cups Swanson's* vegetable broth

1 cup tomato juice or V-8 juice

Dice onion, potato, and other vegetables of your choice. Heat oil in a large skillet over low heat. Add the vegetables and simmer about 15 minutes, until onion is soft and golden. Add seasonings and stock of your choice and bring to a boil, simmering another 15 minutes. Remove from heat. When cool, blend in blender; if too thick, add more stock or juice. This soup keeps well in the fridge. As days go by, add more liquid to thin if needed. *Tip:* Simply use more vegetables, stock, and spices if you are cooking for more people. *Suggestion:* Cauliflower, tomatoes, corn, and watercress make excellent additions.

Nutritional Analysis: *for 1 serving {850 g}*

Calories 446   Calories from fat 84

Nutrient:	% Calories from:	Nutrient:	% Calories from:
Total fat 9 g	18 %	Total carbohydrate 80 g	68 %
Saturated fat 1 g	1 %	Dietary fiber 17 g	
Cholesterol 0 mg		Sugars 17 g	
Sodium 1,326 mg		Protein 16 g	14 %

% Daily:

Vitamin A, 218 %; Vitamin C, 334 %; Calcium, 24 %; Iron, 48 %   11

PAUL ANKA

PAUL ANKA
Tabouli My Way

4 Servings

½ cup dry bulgur* wheat
3 bunches fresh parsley
2 tomatoes
1 ounce shallots or scallions
1 fresh garlic clove
2 tablespoons fresh lemon juice
2 tablespoons olive oil
½ teaspoon salt
½ teaspoon black pepper

Soak bulgur wheat in water for 2 hours. Meanwhile, wash, stem, and chop fine 3 bunches of parsley. Dice tomatoes and put into medium mixing bowl with the parsley. Squeeze excess water from bulgur and toss with parsley-and-tomato mixture. Dice scallion bulbs and some of the green tops and add to mixture, along with minced garlic. Squeeze lemon juice over salad and dribble olive oil. Toss well, using two spoons. Add salt and pepper to taste. *Suggestion:* Serve with quartered pita bread or atop romaine lettuce leaves.

*Note: For a lighter tabouli, use 1 cup bulgur wheat.

Nutritional Analysis: *for 1 serving {134 g}*

Calories 153   Calories from fat 67

Nutrient: % Calories from:		Nutrient: % Calories from:	
Total fat 7 g	41%	Total carbohydrate 20 g	50 %
Saturated fat 1 g	6 %	Dietary fiber 5 g	
Cholesterol 0 mg		Sugars 2 g	
Sodium 294 mg		Protein 4 g	10 %

% Daily:
Vitamin A, 29 %; Vitamin C, 98 %; Calcium, 6 %; Iron, 16 %

DESI ARNAZ JR.

DESI ARNAZ JR.
☆ Desi and Amy's Pasta Delight

2 Servings

5 tablespoons Heart Beat* canola oil

¼ cup fresh chives, chopped

3 garlic cloves, peeled and minced

1 cup chopped broccoli

1 cup chopped asparagus

2 cups chopped Chinese cabbage

1 pound whole-wheat pasta, boiled and drained

¾ cup tomato chunks

1 ounce* fresh cilantro (about a handful)

1 ounce* fresh dillweed (about a handful)

2 teaspoons fresh lime juice (or to taste)

Simmer the chives and garlic in oil in a wok for about 2 minutes. Turn heat to medium-high and add broccoli, asparagus, and Chinese cabbage, stirring frequently. Add a little water if mixture seems too dry. When broccoli turns dark green—after about 3 minutes—add fresh cooked pasta (we like angel hair!). Throw in a handful each of chopped tomatoes, cilantro, and dill. Stir and remove from heat. Allow it to rest 2 minutes while you get the dishes out of the cabinet. Spoon pasta and sauce onto plates and squeeze fresh lime juice all over it. Eat it!

Nutritional Analysis   *for 1 serving {880 g}*
Calories 722   Calories from fat 347

Nutrient: % Calories from:		Nutrient: % Calories from:	
Total fat 39 g	45 %	Total carbohydrate 80 g	41 %
Saturated fat 3 g	3 %	Dietary fiber 14 g	
Cholesterol 0 mg		Sugars 11 g	
Sodium 254 mg		Protein 26 g	13 %

% Daily:
Vitamin A, 71 %; Vitamin C, 489 %; Calcium, 42 %; Iron, 42 %

(PHOTO: DANA GLUCKSTEIN)

ED ASNER

ED ASNER
Balsamic Roasted New Potatoes

6 Servings

2 tablespoons olive oil

2 pounds potatoes (washed, patted dry, and quartered)

4 garlic cloves, minced

1 tablespoon minced shallot

1 teaspoon fresh thyme

1 teaspoon minced rosemary

⅛ teaspoon freshly ground nutmeg

¼ cup balsamic vinegar

½ teaspoon* salt

½ teaspoon* black pepper

Preheat oven to 400°F. Heat olive oil in a 12-inch skillet over medium-high heat. Add potatoes, garlic, and shallot. Toss until well mixed. Add thyme, rosemary, and nutmeg. Toss well again.

When potatoes are hot, spread them onto a baking sheet in a single layer. (Can be made hours in advance to this point). Place sheet on rack in lower third of oven. Roast until golden and just tender, about 25 minutes, turning once halfway. Add vinegar. Toss well. Season to taste with salt and pepper. Return to oven until sizzling, or about 7 minutes. Serve immediately.

Nutritional Analysis   *for 1 serving {172 g}*

Calories 167   Calories from fat 43

Nutrient:	*% Calories from:*	*Nutrient:*	*% Calories from:*
Total fat 5 g	25 %	Total carbohydrate 29 g	67%
Saturated fat 1 g	3%	Dietary fiber 3 g	
Cholesterol 0 mg		Sugars 0 g	
Sodium 191 mg		Protein 4 g	8 %

% Daily:

Vitamin A, 2 %; Vitamin C, 47 %; Calcium, 3 %; Iron, 16 %

ANNE BANCROFT AND MEL BROOKS

ANNE BANCROFT AND MEL BROOKS
Mango–Black-Bean Sauce Over Rice

4 Servings

1 tablespoon olive oil

2 large onions, chopped

1 large carrot, chopped fine

3 garlic cloves, minced

¼ teaspoon cumin, ground

¼ teaspoon coriander, ground

¼ teaspoon chili powder

1 large bunch fresh cilantro (6 ounces*)

1 tablespoon peeled and grated gingerroot

3 cups Swansons* vegetable broth or water

2 tablespoons arrowroot or cornstarch

Half a red or yellow bell pepper (to make 2 tablespoons when roasted and chopped)

1½ ripe mangoes

2 cups cooked black beans

2 tablespoons* lime juice

3 cups long-grain brown rice, cooked

Sauté onions, carrot, and garlic with spices until veggies are just softened. Reserve a few sprigs of the cilantro for garnish and chop the remainder, reserving 2 tablespoons. Add cilantro, grated ginger, and vegetable broth (or water) to vegetables and bring to a boil. Dissolve arrowroot (or cornstarch) in 2 tablespoons water, and add it to the sauce in a thin stream. Cook until slightly thickened; lower heat and simmer twenty minutes. Roast the bell pepper half under the broiler until skin is blistery and starting to brown all over. Cool and dice. Peel and dice mangos. Add mango, beans, roasted pepper and remaining cilantro to vegetable mixture. Bring to a boil. Reduce heat and let cook until mango softens. Serve over brown rice. Sprinkle lime juice on top and garnish with sprigs of cilantro.

Suggestion: Serve with corn tortillas or muffins.

Nutritional Analysis   *for 1 serving {493 g}*

Calories 434   Calories from fat 53

Nutrient: % Calories from:		Nutrient: % Calories from:	
Total fat 6 g	12 %	Total carbohydrate 83 g	75 %
Saturated fat 1 g	2 %	Dietary fiber 10 g	
Cholesterol 0 mg		Sugars 15 g	
Sodium 31 mg		Protein 14 g	13 %

% Daily:

Vitamin A, 93 %; Vitamin C, 60 %; Calcium, 12 %; Iron, 21 %

CAROL BURNETT

CAROL BURNETT
☆ Vegetable Medley

4 Servings

1½ cups zucchini (1 large or 2 small)

1 pound canned corn or kernels from 2 ears fresh corn

⅓ pound fresh mushrooms

2 or 3 ripe tomatoes

6 or 8 scallions

2 tablespoons butter

½ teaspoon salt*

½ teaspoon pepper*

Chop zucchini; drain corn; slice mushrooms. Core and peel the tomatoes and cut into large cubes. Chop scallions in 1-inch pieces. Melt butter in skillet. Add zucchini, corn, mushrooms, and salt and pepper to taste. Cook 1 minute, stirring to coat and mix well. Add scallions, cover, and cook about 1 minute more. Add tomatoes, cover, and cook about 5 minutes, stirring occasionally. Serve while hot.
Suggestion: Garnish with fresh herbs.

Nutritional Analysis   *for 1 serving {328 g}*

Calories 197   Calories from fat 67

Nutrient: % Calories from:		Nutrient: % Calories from:	
Total fat 7 g	30 %	Total carbohydrate 33 g	60 %
Saturated fat 4 g	16 %	Dietary fiber 4 g	
Cholesterol 16 mg		Sugars 8 g	
Sodium 706 mg		Protein 6 g	10 %

% Daily:

Vitamin A, 15 %; Vitamin C, 61 %; Calcium, 4 %; Iron, 13 %

(PHOTO: GARY BERNSTEIN © 1992)

DYAN CANNON

DYAN CANNON

☆ Broccoli-Farfel Stuffing

4 Servings

3 tablespoons margarine

1 cup chopped onions

½ pound mushrooms, coarsely chopped

2 garlic cloves, crushed

10 ounces frozen broccoli, thawed

1½ cups matzoh meal farfel

1 egg

1 egg yolk

1 teaspoon salt

2 teaspoons fresh basil, chopped (or one teaspoon dry)

⅛ teaspoon black pepper

Melt margarine in a skillet. Sauté chopped onions until soft. Add mushrooms and garlic; sauté until most of the liquid has evaporated. Transfer to medium bowl and allow to cool. Stir in chopped broccoli & farfel. Mix egg and egg yolk and add to broccoli-farfel mixture. Stir in seasonings. Put mixture into a casserole dish and bake at 350°F for 30 to 40 minutes or until done.

Nutritional Analysis *for 1 serving {224 g}*

Calories 228   Calories from fat 112

Nutrient:	*% Calories from:*	*Nutrient:*	*% Calories from:*
Total fat 12 g	40 %	Total carbohydrate 33 g	47 %
Saturated fat 2 g	8 %	Dietary fiber 3 g	
Cholesterol 107 mg		Sugars 2 g	
Sodium 686 mg		Protein 9 g	13 %

% Daily:

Vitamin A, 21 %; Vitamin C, 9 %; Calcium, 3 %; Iron, 6 %

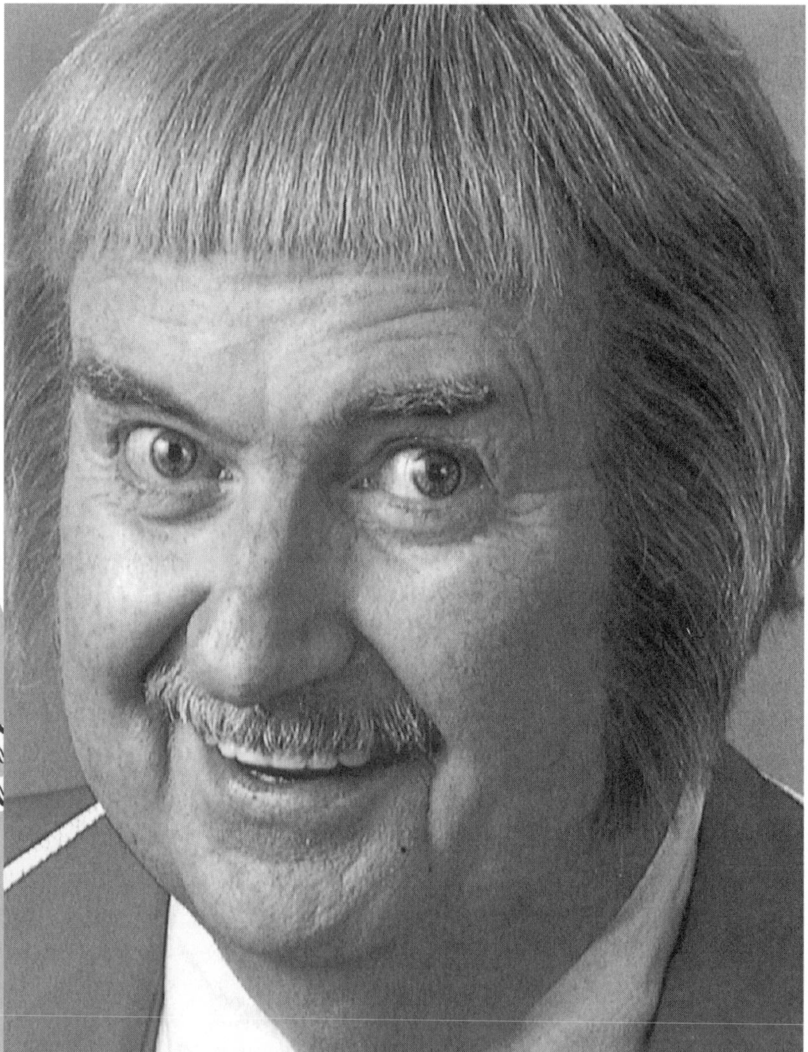

CAPTAIN KANGAROO

CAPTAIN KANGAROO
☆ Vegetable Casserole

6 Servings

4 tablespoons butter
1 teaspoon salt
¼ teaspoon black pepper
1 teaspoon paprika
1 large onion
4 large, firm tomatoes
2 medium potatoes
2 celery stalks
2 medium carrots

Preheat oven to 375°F. Butter a casserole dish, reserving 1 tablespoonful. Combine seasonings in a small bowl. Slice onion and tomatoes into 1/2-inch slices. Dice potatoes and celery; slice carrots. Layer the veggies into the casserole dish, sprinkling each layer with seasoning mixture. Dot with remaining butter, cover, and bake for 1 hour or until tender. Fantastic!

Nutritional Analysis   *for 1 serving {286 g}*
Calories 181   Calories from fat 74

Nutrient:	*% Calories from:*	*Nutrient:*	*% Calories from:*
Total fat 8 g	38 %	Total carbohydrate 26 g	54 %
Saturated fat 5 g	23 %	Dietary fiber 5 g	
Cholesterol 20 mg		Sugars 6 g	
Sodium 490 mg		Protein 4 g	8 %

% Daily:
Vitamin A, 114 %; Vitamin C, 64 %; Calcium, 5 %; Iron, 11 %   25

LYNDA CARTER

LYNDA CARTER
☆ Caesar Salad

4 Servings

½ teaspoon* salt

4 garlic cloves, peeled and pressed

A grating of black pepper (1/2 teaspoon*)

8 anchovy fillets

Juice of 1 lemon (1/4 cup*)

2½ tablespoons Worcestershire sauce

1 tablespoon Grey Poupon Dijon mustard

6 tablespoons* olive oil

2 tablespoons* red wine vinegar

6 cups romaine lettuce

1 egg

½ cup croutons

3 tablespoons grated Parmesan cheese

*amount not specified

Salt the bottom of a wooden salad bowl. Add garlic, black pepper, and anchovies, working it into a paste. Add lemon juice, Worcestershire, and mustard. Work into bowl, adding pepper to taste. Shake oil and vinegar together vigorously. Sprinkle on sides of bowl. Break up lettuce and place in bowl. In simmering water, cook egg gently for 1–1 1/2 minutes; drop egg from shell into bowl. Add croutons and Parmesan cheese, tossing thoroughly. Serve immediately.

Nutritional Analysis   *for 1 serving {199 g}*
Calories 470   Calories from fat 402

Nutrient:	% Calories from:	Nutrient:	% Calories from:
Total fat 45 g	85 %	Total carbohydrate 10 g	8 %
Saturated fat 7 g	13 %	Dietary fiber 2 g	
Cholesterol 64 mg		Sugars 2 g	
Sodium 890 mg		Protein 8 g	7 %

% Daily:
Vitamin A, 26 %; Vitamin C, 64 %; Calcium, 14 %; Iron, 14 %

JOANNA CASSIDY

JOANNA CASSIDY
Hot 'n' Spicy Okra

4 Servings

2 pounds fresh okra

1 teaspoon* Mongolian hot oil, House of Tsang*

2 tablespoons* fresh rosemary

½ teaspoon* salt

½ teaspoon* white pepper

Wash okra thoroughly. Shake in a bag with a good shake of Mongolian Hot Oil, a handful of chopped fresh rosemary, and salt and pepper to taste. Skewer and grill.

Nutritional Analysis *for 1 serving {231 g}*

Calories 84   Calories from fat 14

Nutrient:	% Calories from:	Nutrient:	% Calories from:
Total fat 2 g	15 %	Total carbohydrate 17 g	68 %
Saturated fat 0 g	2 %	Dietary fiber 3 g	
Cholesterol 0 mg		Sugars 5 g	
Sodium 298 mg		Protein 4 g	17 %

% Daily:

Vitamin A, 13 %; Vitamin C, 62 %; Calcium, 15 %; Iron, 6 %

PHOEBE CATES

☆ Saffron Risotto With Wild Mushrooms and Arugula

4 Servings

2 cups Swansons* vegetable stock

5 grams saffron (pinch)

4 tablespoons butter

6 ounces minced onion (1 small)

1 garlic clove, crushed

1½ cups Arborio rice

½ cup dry white wine

2 tablespoons olive oil

4 ounces fresh arugula (1 packed cup)

6 ounces fresh wild mushrooms (1 cup)

½ teaspoon* salt

½ teaspoon* white pepper

½ cups grated Parmesan or pecorino cheese

Heat the stock in a small saucepan, add a pinch of saffron strands and allow to infuse for 10 minutes. Melt the butter in a medium skillet. Sauté the onion and garlic for 5 minutes over low heat or until soft. Add the rice and stir over medium heat for 2–3 minutes, or until it is opaque. Pour in wine; simmer rapidly until most of the liquid has evaporated. Add a third of the warm stock, stir once, and simmer very gently over low heat until liquid is absorbed. Repeat this process twice with the remaining stock until the rice is tender, about 25 minutes. Just before the rice is cooked, in a small skillet, heat the oil and stir-fry the mushrooms about 4–5 minutes. Add arugula, stirring briefly until just wilted. Stir the mushrooms and arugula into the rice, along with the Parmesan cheese, salt, and plenty of pepper. Serve immediately.

Nutritional Analysis *for 1 serving {250 g}*

Calories 525   Calories from fat 217

Nutrient:	% Calories from:	Nutrient:	% Calories from:
Total fat 24 g	40 %	Total carbohydrate 65 g	47 %
Saturated fat 10 g	17 %	Dietary fiber 1 g	
Cholesterol 41 mg		Sugars 1 g	
Sodium 654 mg		Protein 13 g	10 %

% Daily:

Vitamin A, 20 %; Vitamin C, 5 %; Calcium, 23 %; Iron, 4 %

MARGE CHAMPION

Marge and Daniel's Red Lentil Soup

2 Servings

5 cups* water

8 ounces dried lentils

1 bay leaf, broken

2 teaspoons olive oil

3 garlic cloves, peeled and minced

2 cups onion, peeled and chopped

1½ cups chopped carrots

¾ cup chopped celery

1 cup tomatoes, chopped or puréed

1 tablespoon fresh rosemary

¼ –½ teaspoon red pepper flakes

1 tablespoon white vinegar

½ teaspoon* salt

½ teaspoon* black pepper

4 teaspoons* fresh lemon juice

Bring water, lentils, and bay leaf to a boil, partly covered. Reduce heat, simmering until soft (about 10–15 minutes). Meanwhile, heat oil in skillet on medium-high. Sauté garlic and onions to a nice golden brown; add carrots and celery. Sauté until vegetables soften. Add tomatoes, rosemary, hot red pepper flakes, and vinegar; reduce heat to simmer. When lentils are tender, drain, reserving cooking liquid. Discard bay leaf. Purée half of the lentils with some of the cooking liquid. Add puréed lentils and whole lentils to the vegetable mixture, along with enough of the cooking liquid to make a thick soup. Heat thoroughly; add salt and pepper to taste. Serve with additional red pepper flakes and a splash of lemon.

Nutritional Analysis   *for 1 serving {1209 g}*

Calories 572   Calories from fat 53

Nutrient: % Calories from:		Nutrient: % Calories from:	
Total fat 6 g	9 %	Total carbohydrate 107 g	73 %
Saturated fat 1 g	1 %	Dietary fiber 15 g	
Cholesterol 0 mg		Sugars 24 g	
Sodium 696 mg		Protein 27 g	18 %

% Daily:

Vitamin A, 462 %; Vitamin C, 92 %; Calcium, 26 %; Iron, 63 %   33

MARGE CHAMPION

Roasted Brussels Sprouts

2 Servings

12 ounces* fresh Brussels sprouts
1 teaspoon* olive oil
¼ teaspoon* kosher salt

Preheat oven to 375°F. Cut Brussels sprouts in half and spread halves on baking sheet. Drizzle lightly with oil. Sprinkle with salt. Bake on middle rack until edges begin to brown and sprouts get tender. Serve hot or at room temperature.

Nutritional Analysis   *for 1 serving {173 g}*

Calories 93   Calories from fat 25

Nutrient:	% Calories from:	Nutrient:	% Calories from:
Total fat 3 g	23 %	Total carbohydrate 15 g	56 %
Saturated fat 0 g	3 %	Dietary fiber 7 g	
Cholesterol 0 mg		Sugars 4 g	
Sodium 329 mg		Protein 6 g	21 %

% Daily:
Vitamin A, 15 %; Vitamin C, 241 %; Calcium, 7 %; Iron, 13 %

MARGE CHAMPION

☆ Stuffed Nutted Squash

2 Servings

1 acorn squash

¾ cup pecan halves, chopped

1 small onion, chopped

1 tablespoon fresh parsley, chopped

½ cup dried Craneberry's* cranberries

1 cup orange juice

Preheat oven to 375°F. Cut squash in half and scrape out seeds. Mix pecans with onion, parsley, and dried cranberries. Set squash halves on a baking sheet and stuff with nut mixture. Pour orange juice into each half. Bake 45 minutes to an hour, or until fork easily pierces flesh. Serve hot and enjoy. Tip: Line baking sheet with aluminum foil or parchment paper to prevent sticking.

Nutritional Analysis   *for 1 serving {368 g}*

Calories 504   Calories from fat 251

Nutrient:	% Calories from:	Nutrient:	% Calories from:
Total fat 28 g	47 %	Total carbohydrate 64 g	48 %
Saturated fat 2 g	4 %	Dietary fiber 9 g	
Cholesterol 0 mg		Sugars 20 g	
Sodium 9 mg		Protein 6 g	5 %

% Daily:

Vitamin A, 9 %; Vitamin C, 136 %; Calcium, 9 %; Iron, 13 %

CHEVY CHASE

☆ Chevy and Jayni's Vegetable Lasagne

8 Servings

16 ounces curly edge lasagne (1 box)

2 pounds broccoli, chopped

2 teaspoons olive oil

4 medium zucchini, chopped

1 medium onion, chopped

2 garlic cloves, peeled and minced

1 28-ounce can whole tomatoes

½ teaspoon salt*

3 cups (24 ounces) skim milk ricotta cheese

1 teaspoon oregano

12 ounces mozzarella cheese

1 16-ounce jar Health Valley* spaghetti sauce

½ cup grated Parmesan cheese

Preheat oven 350°F. Precook lasagne noodles. Steam broccoli 2 minutes. Heat the olive oil and sauté chopped zucchini together with onion, garlic, steamed broccoli, tomatoes, and salt over high heat about 5 minutes. In a large bowl combine ricotta, oregano and shredded mozzarella thoroughly. Heat spaghetti sauce. In a baking dish (about 13 by 9 inches), spread half of the sauce. Layer noodles, tomato-veggie mixture, and cheese mixture. Repeat layers, ending with a layer of lasagne and the other half of the spaghetti sauce on top. Bake 45 minutes. *Suggestion:* Sprinkle on extra Parmesan if desired. Serve with crusty bread and a crunchy green salad.

Nutritional Analysis   *for 1 serving {546 g}*
Calories 597   Calories from fat 203

Nutrient: % Calories from:	Nutrient: % Calories from:
Total fat 23 g 33 %	Total carbohydrate 66 g 43 %
Saturated fat 12 g 17 %	Dietary fiber 5 g
Cholesterol 71 mg	Sugars 10 g
Sodium 749 mg	Protein 35 g 23 %

% Daily:

Vitamin A, 52 %; Vitamin C, 225 %; Calcium, 70 %; Iron, 29 %;   37

JULIE CHRISTIE

JULIE CHRISTIE
☆ Vegetable Cottage Pie

8 Servings

2 pounds potatoes, diced

½ cup milk

2 large onions, peeled and chopped

2 garlic cloves, peeled and minced

1 teaspoon corn oil

1 teaspoon Marmite* yeast spread (or 2 tsp brewer's yeast)

14 ounces canned whole tomatoes

1¼ cups white wine

2 tablespoons* mixed herbs (handful)

⅓ cup minced celery

¼ teaspoon chili powder or 1 small chili pepper

1 pound mixed nuts, finely milled

½ teaspoon* salt

¼ pound Cheddar cheese, grated

Steam, boil, or microwave potatoes; when tender, mash with milk. Preheat oven to 375°F. Sauté onion and garlic in oil; add yeast and tomatoes and simmer until yeast is dissolved. Add wine, herbs, celery, chili powder (use a small, dried whole chili if you like it hot), and salt. Stir into bowl with nuts and mix thoroughly. Put in a baking dish and cover with mashed potatoes. Sprinkle top with cheese. Bake as long as it takes to brown top nicely, about 30 minutes.

Nutritional Analysis   *for 1 serving {341 g}*

Calories 559   Calories from fat 343

Nutrient: % Calories from:		Nutrient: % Calories from:	
Total fat 38 g	59 %	Total carbohydrate 35 g	24 %
Saturated fat 8 g	13 %	Dietary fiber 10 g	
Cholesterol 17 mg		Sugars 4 g	
Sodium 259 mg		Protein 18 g	13 %

% Daily:

Vitamin A, 11 %; Vitamin C, 43 %; Calcium, 29 %; Iron, 42 %   39

JUDY COLLINS

Grilled Veggies

2 Servings

1 portion* raspberry goat cheese marinade

4 ounces* onion (about 1 small)

6 ounces* mushrooms (about 1 cup)

4 ounces* zucchini (about 1 cup)

4 ounces* yellow squash (about 1 cup)

8 ounces* eggplant

1 tablespoon soy sauce

1 garlic clove*, peeled and minced

5 grams* (1 pinch) mustard powder

½ teaspoon* ginger

½ teaspoon* Poultry Magic poultry seasoning

½ teaspoon* salt

½ teaspoon* black pepper

½ tablespoon* olive oil

Raspberry Goat Cheese Marinade

1 ounce goat cheese

4 tablespoons raspberry preserves

Mix together thoroughly.

First make marinade. Crumble the goat cheese into the raspberry preserves and mix thoroughly. Cut the vegetables in large slices and marinate at least 1 hour. (Leave the peelings on to hold the veggies together during grilling.) In a small bowl, combine soy sauce, garlic, mustard, ginger, Poultry Magic, salt, and pepper. Heat oil in skillet. Transfer veggies from marinade to skillet, add soy sauce mixture, and sauté until al dente. Finally, skewer and grill until just brown. Scrumptious!

Nutritional Analysis   *for 1 serving {392 g}*

Calories 162   Calories from fat 63

Nutrient:	*% Calories from:*	*Nutrient:*	*% Calories from:*
Total fat 7 g	34 %	Total carbohydrate 22 g	49 %
Saturated fat 1 g	4 %	Dietary fiber 2 g	
Cholesterol 1 mg		Sugars 7 g	
Sodium 1,008 mg		Protein 8 g	17 %

% Daily:

Vitamin A, 3 %; Vitamin C, 18 %; Calcium, 7 %; Iron, 11 %

CAROL CONNORS

☆ Aunt Carol's Banana Wanana Nutty Wuddy Bread

12 Servings

1 tsp butter

1 tsp flour

1 ¾ cups flour

2 tsps baking powder

½ tsp baking soda

½ tsp cinnamon

½ tsp nutmeg

½ tsp salt

*2 ripe bananas, mashed
(1 cup)*

¾ cups sugar

2 eggs

¼ cups butter

¼ cup milk

1 cup almonds, chopped

6 ounces butterscotch chips

½ cup butter, softened

3 ounces cream cheese

1 tsp vanilla

1 cup powdered sugar

Preheat oven to 350F. Grease and flour 2 loaf pans. Sift flour, baking powder and soda, cinnamon, nutmeg and salt together. Combine bananas, sugar, eggs, and melted butter. Alternately blend in flour mixture and milk. Stir in nuts and butterscotch pieces, reserving some for topping. Turn mixture into prepared loaf pans. Sprinkle remaining nuts and butterscotch pieces on top. Bake for about 40 minutes. For frosting, cream butter together with cream cheese until smooth. Beat in vanilla and powdered sugar to taste. When cake has cooled, drizzle frosting on top.

Nutritional Analysis for 1 serving {130 g}
Calories 445   Calories from Fat 216

Nutrient:	% Calories from:	Nutrient:	% Calories from:
Total fat 24 g	48 %	Total carbohydrate 53 g	46 %
Saturated fat 10 g	19 %	Dietary fiber 2 g	
Cholesterol 76 mg		Sugars 26 g	
Sodium 352 mg		Protein 7 g	6 %

% Daily:
Vitamin A, 16 %; Vitamin C, 5 %; Calcium, 8 %; Iron, 9 %

Best Wishes
Tim Conway

TIM CONWAY

TIM CONWAY

☆ Chicory and Kidney Bean Salad

4 Servings

2 heads of chicory

1 16-ounce can red kidney beans

1 medium onion, minced

3 tablespoons olive oil

2 tablespoons red wine vinegar

½ teaspoon* salt

½ teaspoon* white pepper

I like this salad best with pita, Italian, or French bread. It's yummy. Once you get the hang of it, you can adjust the amounts to suit your own taste buds. ENJOY!!

Wash the chicory. Discard the tougher outer leaves (unless you're an antelope). Spin it in a lettuce dryer or pat leaves dry. Pour kidney beans and liquid into a bowl and mash lovingly with a potato masher, forming a paste. Fold in onion, oil, vinegar, and salt and pepper to taste. Put chicory leaves into a salad bowl, add the bean mixture, and toss until it looks suitable for serving.

Nutritional Analysis   *for 1 serving {389 g}*

Calories 257   Calories from fat 102

Nutrient:	**% Calories from:**	**Nutrient:**	**% Calories from:**
Total fat 11 g	37 %	Total carbohydrate 32 g	47 %
Saturated fat 2 g	5 %	Dietary fiber 11 g	
Cholesterol 0 mg		Sugars 3 g	
Sodium 394 mg		Protein 11 g	16 %

% Daily:

Vitamin A, 91 %; Vitamin C, 100 %; Calcium, 27 %; Iron, 23 %   45

DORIS DAY

DORIS DAY
☆ Sicilian Cheese Casserole

6 Servings

1 cup uncooked tiny shell pasta

1 medium eggplant, pared and cut in ½-inch cubes

1 small onion, chopped

3 tablespoons olive oil

3 ounces tomato sauce

2 ounces fresh parsley, chopped

2 tablespoons lemon juice

½ cup ripe olives, halved and pitted

1½ cups grated Parmesan cheese

1 teaspoon salt

1 teaspoon black pepper

½ teaspoon basil

½ teaspoon marjoram

½ pound Monterey Jack cheese, sliced thinly

2 garlic cloves*, crushed

Preheat oven to 375°F. Cook tiny shell pasta and drain. Sauté eggplant, onion and garlic in oil over medium heat until tender. Combine with pasta, tomato sauce, parsley, lemon juice, olives, Parmesan, and seasonings. Transfer to a 2-quart baking dish. Top with sliced Monterey Jack and bake uncovered for 30 minutes.

Nutritional Analysis   *for 1 serving {215 g}*

Calories 450   Calories from fat 272

Nutrient: % Calories from:		Nutrient: % Calories from:	
Total fat 30 g	59 %	Total carbohydrate 23 g	20 %
Saturated fat 13 g	26 %	Dietary fiber 1 g	
Cholesterol 53 mg		Sugars 0 g	
Sodium 1,404 mg		Protein 24 g	21 %

% Daily:

Vitamin A, 23 %; Vitamin C, 28 %; Calcium, 67 %; Iron, 13 %

LYNDA DAY-GEORGE

LYNDA DAY-GEORGE

☆ Potatoes Lynda

4 Servings

*4 medium, evenly shaped
potatoes*

1 teaspoon salt

3 tablespoons butter, melted

*2–3 tablespoons chopped
fresh herbs (e.g., parsley,
chives, sage, thyme, jalapeño
peppers)*

*4 tablespoons grated Cheddar
cheese*

*1½ tablespoons grated
Parmesan cheese*

2 teaspoons paprika

Preheat oven to 425°F. Scrub the potatoes. Cut across each potato in thin slices, but not all the way through, leaving about 1/4 inch at the base, so the potato stays together. Put potatoes on a baking dish. Mix salt, melted butter, and most of the herbs and drizzle into grooves. Sprinkle remaining herbs on top. Bake for 45–50 minutes. Remove from oven, spinkle with cheeses, and paprika. Return to oven for about 12 minutes or until golden brown. Serve as a side dish or main meal with salad. *Variation:* Use 1 1/2 teaspoons caraway seed or cumin in place of herbs. *Tip:* Lay a wooden spoon handle alongside the potato to prevent the knife from cutting all the way through.

Nutritional Analysis *for 1 serving {262 g}*

Calories 270   Calories from fat 113

Nutrient:	% Calories from:	Nutrient:	% Calories from:
Total fat 13 g	39 %	Total carbohydrate 33 g	47 %
Saturated fat 7 g	23 %	Dietary fiber 7 g	
Cholesterol 32 mg		Sugars 0 g	
Sodium 735 mg		Protein 10 g	14 %

% Daily:

Vitamin A, 23 %; Vitamin C, 52 %; Calcium, 27 %; Iron, 65 %

DOM DELUISE

DOM DELUISE

☆ Stuffed and Rolled Eggplant Marinara

8 Servings

3 tablespoons olive oil

5 garlic cloves, peeled and minced

6 ounces tomato paste

5 pounds tomatoes, blanched and peeled

10 basil leaves, shredded into small pieces

½ teaspoon black pepper

4 ounces grated Parmesan cheese

2 large eggplants, peeled

1 ounce parsley, chopped fine

1 pound ricotta cheese

½ cup all-purpose flour

2 eggs, beaten

3 tablespoons olive oil

½ pound mozzarella cheese, sliced thin

4 ounces grated Parmesan cheese

For marinara sauce: Heat olive oil in a frying pan and sauté garlic. Stir in tomato paste and tomatoes. Cook over medium heat for 20–30 minutes, stirring occasionally. Sprinkle basil on top. Add pepper and grated cheese to taste. Remove from heat. For stuffed eggplant: Preheat oven to 350°F. Stir parsley into ricotta and set aside. Slice peeled eggplants lengthwise in 1/4-inch slices. Dredge in flour, dip in beaten eggs, and fry until golden brown. Pat dry with paper towels. Place a mozzarella slice and a scoop of ricotta in the middle of each eggplant slice. Roll up and place, seam side down, in a greased shallow baking pan. Cover with marinara sauce. Bake 25–30 minutes. Allow to set up before serving. Garnish with additional parsley and grated Parmesan. *Suggestion:* Serve with salad and bread or pasta. *Variation:* Add 4 tablespoons sun-dried tomatoes to marinara sauce when adding tomato paste.

Nutritional Analysis *for 1 serving {564 g}*

Calories 567   Calories from fat 320

Nutrient:	% Calories from:	Nutrient:	% Calories from:
Total fat 36 g	55 %	Total carbohydrate 34 g	24 %
Saturated fat 16 g	24 %	Dietary fiber 5 g	
Cholesterol 129 mg		Sugars 9 g	
Sodium 799 mg		Protein 31 g	21 %

% Daily:

Vitamin A, 49 %; Vitamin C, 117 %; Calcium, 72 %; Iron, 20 %

PHYLLIS DILLER

PHYLLIS DILLER

☆ Parmesan Eggplant Casserole

6 Servings

1 cup butter
2 large eggplants
1 cup minced onion
1 bell pepper, minced
2 teaspoons parsley, minced
1 ¾ cup grated Parmesan cheese
1 1-pound can stewed tomatoes
½ teaspoon* salt
½ teaspoon* black pepper
⅓ cup* cracker meal
⅓ teaspoon* paprika
½ cup melted butter

Preheat oven to 350°F. Grease a casserole dish with some of the butter. Peel eggplants and chop coarsely. Melt butter in skillet, add eggplant, onions, and pepper, and simmer 15 minutes. Add parsley, 2/3 of the Parmesan and all of the tomatoes. Simmer 5 more minutes, add salt and pepper, and place in casserole. Combine cracker meal, paprika, and remaining Parmesan, and sprinkle on top of casserole. Drizzle with melted butter. Bake for 20 minutes. *Suggestion:* Great with crusty bread and leafy salad. *Tip:* Freezes well before baking.

Nutritional Analysis   *for 1 serving {341 g}*
Calories 627   Calories from fat 495

Nutrient:	% Calories from:	Nutrient:	% Calories from:
Total fat 55 g	77 %	Total carbohydrate 22 g	13 %
Saturated fat 34 g	48 %	Dietary fiber 2 g	
Cholesterol 147 mg		Sugars 3 g	
Sodium 1,552 mg		Protein 15 g	10 %

% Daily:
Vitamin A, 58 %; Vitamin C, 67 %; Calcium, 46 %; Iron, 11 %

With laughter
+ best wishes
Julia Duffy

JULIA DUFFY

JULIA DUFFY

☆ Herbed Zucchini Latkes with Roasted Peppers

Although I'm not a strict vegetarian, I'm very much opposed to the idea of centering our diets around meat. Those who continue to eat meat should do so sparingly, for the sake of their bodies and our planet.

6 Servings

1 pound zucchini, grated medium fine

½ teaspoon salt

3 tablespoons grated onion

1 large red bell pepper

1 egg, beaten

½ cup grated Parmesan cheese

¼ cup whole milk

1 teaspoon rosemary

1 teaspoon chopped basil

2 teaspoons minced fresh herbs

¼ teaspoon Tabasco sauce

½ teaspoon black pepper

½ tsp salt

½ cup all-purpose flour

1 teaspoon baking powder

3 tablespoons olive oil

½ cup yogurt

Sprinkle zucchini with salt and set aside for 1 hour. Drain and squeeze out excess liquid. Cut bell pepper into quarters, removing seeds. Roast under broiler until skin is blistery and beginning to turn brown all over. When cool enough to handle, remove skin and mince flesh. Mix zucchini, onion, and 2 tablespoons of the minced pepper, and set aside. In a medium mixing bowl, combine egg, cheese, milk, herbs, salt, Tabasco, and pepper to taste. Sift flour and baking powder together. Add veggies to egg mixture, sift flour again, into the veggies, mixing thoroughly. Heat a little oil in a skillet over medium-high heat. Spoon mixture into skillet, pressing to form thin 3-inch round latkes. Lightly brown both sides; drain on absorbent paper. Wipe and add oil as needed. Purée remaining red pepper with yogurt. Serve latkes with a spoonful of pepper sauce on top.

Nutritional Analysis *for 1 serving {195 g}*
Calories 241   Calories from fat 128

Nutrient:	*% Calories from:*	*Nutrient:*	*% Calories from:*
Total fat 14 g	52 %	Total carbohydrate 17 g	27 %
Saturated fat 5 g	19 %	Dietary fiber 1 g	
Cholesterol 53 mg		Sugars 3 g	
Sodium 770 mg		Protein 13 g	21 %

% Daily:
Vitamin A, 10 %; Vitamin C, 14 %; Calcium, 35 %; Iron, 10 %

ROGER EBERT

ROGER EBERT
Dot's Bread Pudding

12 Servings

*4 servings cooking spray
(1 second of spray equals
1 serving)*

1 tablespoon cinnamon

1 teaspoon nutmeg

½ teaspoons ginger

*2 loaves whole-wheat fat-free
bread, day old if possible*

1 cup raisins ("generous
amount")*

½ gallon skim milk

12 grams (12 packets)
Equal* sugar substitute
(optional)*

*1 carton Egg Beaters (or
equivalent amount of any egg
substitute)*

Preheat oven to 375°F. Spray baking dish with cooking spray. In a small bowl combine spices. Tear bread into pieces and cover bottom of dish. Sprinkle generously with raisins and spice mixture. Continue layering with remaining bread, raisins, and spice. In a separate bowl, mix milk, optional sugar substitute, and Egg Beaters or other egg substitute. Pour over bread layers, adjusting amount so that the bread is well moistened but not drenched. Reduce heat to 350°F and bake about 45 minutes or until done. *Variations:* Instead of raisins, use your favorite fruit; try blueberries, raspberries, dried cranberries, peaches, etc. *Suggestion:* For a special treat, serve with nonfat frozen yogurt or with a lemon sauce.

Nutritional Analysis   *for 1 serving {291 g}*

Calories 261   Calories from fat 8

Nutrient:	% Calories from:	Nutrient:	% Calories from:
Total fat 1 g	3 %	Total carbohydrate 44 g	70 %
Saturated fat 0 g	1 %	Dietary fiber 1 g	
Cholesterol 3 mg		Sugars 15 g	
Sodium 536 mg		Protein 17 g	27 %

% Daily:

Vitamin A, 31 %; Vitamin C, 4 %; Calcium, 26 %; Iron, 7 %

ANNE FRANCIS

ANNE FRANCIS
Steamed Veggies

2 Servings

*3 carrots**

1 cup green beans*

*1 small onion, 6 ounces**

*2 medium-large potatoes, 18 ounces**

1 garlic clove, crushed*

1 tablespoon Nucoa Smart Beat* low-fat margarine*

¼ teaspoon salt*

½ teaspoon mixed herbs of your choice*

This quick end-of-day recipe is my most satisfying meal.

Chop all vegetables in 1-inch pieces and steam 10–15 minutes, or until slightly crisp (al dente). While the veggies are steaming, mince fresh garlic clove (or cloves! Yum!!) into a bowl, along with margarine (or butter), herbs, and salt to taste. Mix steamed veggies with "garlic butter" sauce. Serve at once as an entrée or on the side with pasta or salad. If you don't like garlic (obviously I love it!), create your own sauce.

Nutritional Analysis   *for 1 serving {514 g}*
Calories 302   Calories from fat 15

Nutrient: % Calories from:	Nutrient: % Calories from:
Total fat 2 g 5 %	Total carbohydrate 66 g 84 %
Saturated fat 0 g 0 %	Dietary fiber 9 g
Cholesterol 0 mg	Sugars 14 g
Sodium 382 mg	Protein 9 g 11 %

% Daily:
Vitamin A, 316 %; Vitamin C, 116 %; Calcium, 12 %; Iron, 29 %   59

MICKEY GILLEY

MICKEY GILLEY
☆ Marshmallow Sweet Potatoes

6 Servings

4 cups hot mashed sweet potatoes

¼ cup margarine

¼ cup orange juice

½ teaspoon salt

2 cups (4 ounces) miniature marshmallows

Preheat oven to 350°F. To the mashed sweet potatoes, add margarine, orange juice, and salt. Whip in 1 cup of the marshmallows. Place in a 1 1/2 quart casserole and bake for 20 minutes. Top with remaining marshmallows and return to oven until lightly browned. Allow to cool slightly before serving.

Nutritional Analysis   *for 1 serving {130 g}*

Calories 241   Calories from fat 67

Nutrient:	% Calories from:	Nutrient:	% Calories from:
Total fat 7 g	27 %	Total carbohydrate 43 g	70 %
Saturated fat 1 g	5 %	Dietary fiber 2 g	
Cholesterol 0 mg		Sugars 2 g	
Sodium 324 mg		Protein 2 g	3 %

% Daily:

Vitamin A, 10 %; Vitamin C, 27 %; Calcium, 2 %; Iron, 3 %

AMY GRANT
☆ Sugar Cookies

60 Servings (5 dozen cookies)

3 servings cooking spray (3 seconds of spray)
1 cup Crisco
1 cup sugar
2 beaten eggs
2 cups self-rising flour
2 teaspoons sweetened milk

Preheat oven to 375°F. Spray cookie sheet with cooking spray. Cream shortening until soft. Add sugar gradually, creaming after each addition. Blend in beaten eggs and half the flour. Add milk and work in remaining flour, mixing well. Drop by teaspoonfuls onto sprayed cookie sheet. Bake 10–12 minutes. *Variations:* Sprinkle extra sugar on top or decorate with candied fruit, dates, raisins, or nuts. *Tip:* Turn cookie sheet halfway through baking.

Nutritional Analysis *for 1 cookie {13 g}*
Calories 62   Calories from fat 33

Nutrient:	*% Calories from:*	*Nutrient:*	*% Calories from:*
Total fat 4 g	53 %	Total carbohydrate 7 g	42 %
Saturated fat 1 g	13 %	Dietary fiber 1 g	
Cholesterol 50 mg		Sugars 3 g	
Sodium 55 mg		Protein 1 g	4 %

% Daily:
Vitamin A, 4 %; Vitamin C, 0 %; Calcium, 2 %; Iron, 1 %

TIPPI HEDREN

TIPPI HEDREN

☆ Hot Artichoke Dip

20 Servings

1 14-ounce can artichoke hearts
1 cup Kraft mayonnaise
1 garlic clove, minced
4 ounces grated Parmesan cheese

"This tastes outrageously divine!"

Preheat oven to 350°F. Drain artichokes and chop. Mix all ingredients thoroughly. Spread evenly in a 9-inch round pie tin and bake 20–25 minutes. *Suggestion:* Serve buffet style, with chips or crackers—whatever you like.

Nutritional Analysis *for 1 serving {37 g}*
Calories 116   Calories from fat 102

Nutrient:	% Calories from:	Nutrient:	% Calories from:
Total fat 11 g	82 %	Total carbohydrate 2 g	8 %
Saturated fat 3 g	19 %	Dietary fiber 1 g	
Cholesterol 8 mg		Sugars 0 g	
Sodium 181 mg		Protein 3 g	10 %

% Daily:
Vitamin A, 2 %; Vitamin C, 3 %; Calcium, 9 %; Iron, 2 %

☆ Spinach Dip

20 Servings

1 package frozen chopped spinach
8 ounces sour cream
1 cup mayonnaise
½ teaspoon lemon juice
1 teaspoon Italian salad dressing
6 garlic cloves, crushed
1 tablespoon minced parsley
6 minced shallots

Thaw chopped spinach. Press out excess water. Mix all ingredients together in a medium mixing bowl. Transfer to serving dish. *Suggestions:* Great with crackers, chips, and crudités.

Nutritional Analysis *for 1 serving {42 g}*
Calories 114   Calories from fat 109

Nutrient:	% Calories from:	Nutrient:	% Calories from:
Total fat 12 g	89 %	Total carbohydrate 2 g	8 %
Saturated fat 3 g	23 %	Dietary fiber 0 g	
Cholesterol 9 mg		Sugars 0 g	
Sodium 77 mg		Protein 1 g	3 %

% Daily:
Vitamin A, 19 %; Vitamin C, 5 %; Calcium, 4 %; Iron, 2 %

CELESTE HOLM

CELESTE HOLM

☆ Tomato-Orange Cream Soup

6 Servings

1 10¾ -ounce can condensed tomato soup

9 ounces canned tomato juice

3½ ounces orange juice concentrate

2 tablespoons lemon juice

½ cup cream

3 ounces heavy whipped cream

This versatile soup may be served hot or cold, as an appetizer or as dessert. Whip first four ingredients together, then fold in cream. Serve very cold. To serve hot: heat tomato-orange mixture, then add the cream. Serve with generous dollops of whipped cream.

Nutritional Analysis *for 1 serving {155 g}*

Calories 170   from fat 121

Nutrient:	% Calories from:	Nutrient:	% Calories from:
Total fat 13 g	67 %	Total carbohydrate 13 g	28 %
Saturated fat 3 g	17 %	Dietary fiber 1 g	
Cholesterol 47 mg		Sugars 2 g	
Sodium 566 mg		Protein 2 g	5 %

% Daily:

Vitamin A, 12 %; Vitamin C, 70 %; Calcium, 2 %; Iron, 6 %

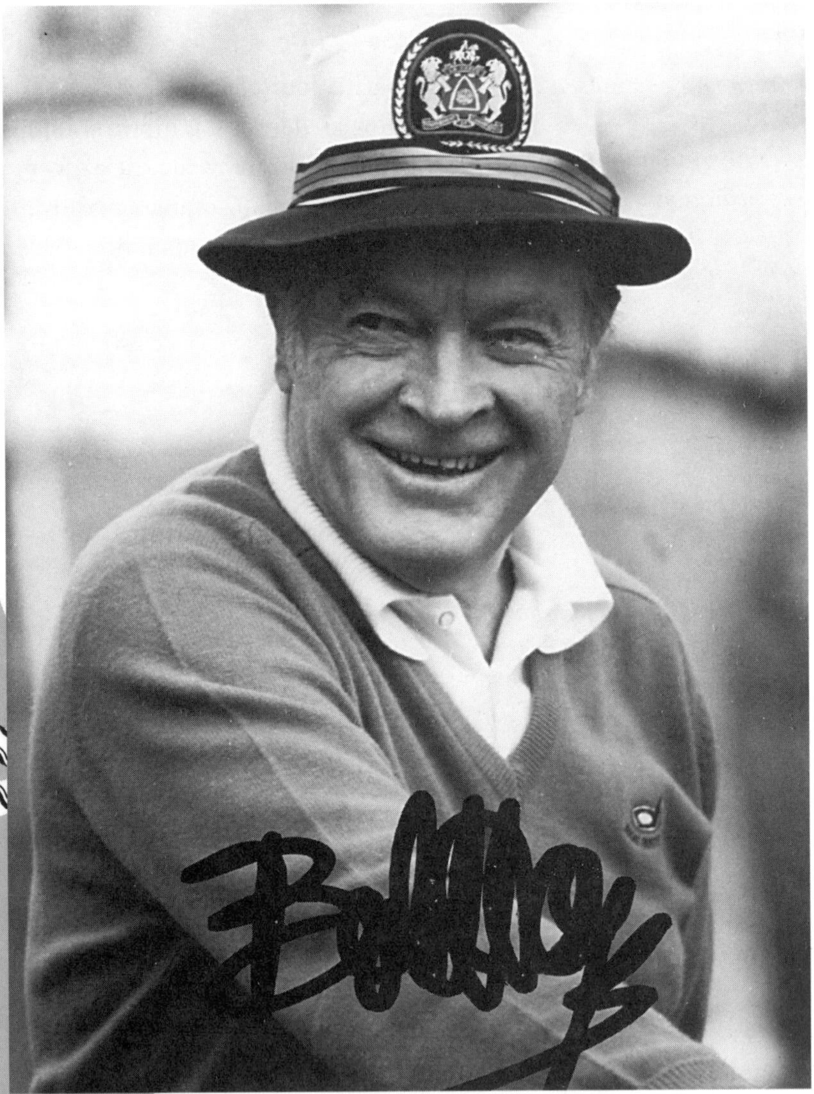

BOB HOPE

BOB HOPE

★ Bob's Favorite Lemon Pie

8 Servings

1 prebaked piecrust

3 egg whites

1 cup sugar

3 tablespoons cornstarch

1 cup water

4 egg yolks, lightly beaten

2 tablespoons butter

1 teaspoon lemon zest (finely grated peel)

4 tablespoons lemon juice (2 or 3 lemons)

⅛ teaspoon salt

2 tablespoons sugar

Prepare crust. Refrigerate egg whites until ready to make meringue. *Pie Filling:* In a saucepan or double boiler, combine sugar and cornstarch, adding water slowly and stirring constantly over medium heat until thick and smooth. Add egg yolks a little at a time while stirring rapidly. Stir in butter, lemon zest, lemon juice, and salt. Reduce heat and cook 2–3 minutes, stirring occasionally. Remove from heat and set aside. *Meringue:* Preheat oven to 325°F. Beat chilled egg whites until frothy. Add the 2 tablespoons of sugar very gradually, beating thoroughly after each addition. Beat until stiff. Spoon lemon filling into prebaked piecrust. Cover with meringue and bake about 15 minutes or until meringue is lightly browned. Cool.

Nutritional Analysis   *for 1 serving {108 g}*

Calories 263   Calories from fat 95

Nutrient: % Calories from:		Nutrient: % Calories from:	
Total fat 11 g	36 %	Total carbohydrate 39 g	59 %
Saturated fat 4 g	14 %	Dietary fiber 0 g	
Cholesterol 114 mg		Sugars 27 g	
Sodium 190 mg		Protein 3 g	5 %

% Daily:

Vitamin A, 19 %; Vitamin C, 1 %; Calcium, 2 %; Iron, 4 %

KIM HUNTER

KIM HUNTER

☆ Givetch

6 Servings

1 cup carrots, sliced thin

1 cup snap beans, 3/4-inch diagonal slices

1 cup potato, diced (optional)

½ cup celery, ½-inch diagonal slices

2 medium tomatoes, peeled and quartered

1 cup zucchini, ½-inch slices

1 cup yellow squash, sliced thin

½ onion, ¼-inch slices

¼ cup each: red and green peppers, in thin strips

3 scallions, ½-inch slices, including green tops

½ head cauliflower, cut in florets

½ cup fresh green peas

1 tablespoon chopped parsley

1 cup vegetable broth

⅓ cup olive oil

3 garlic cloves, minced

2 teaspoons salt

¼ teaspoon crumbled bay leaf

½ teaspoon each rosemary and chili powder

¼ teaspoon thyme

1 teaspoon sesame seeds

Preheat oven to 350°F. Combine all vegetables in a casserole dish; mix gently and set aside. Heat the broth over medium-high heat and add oil, minced garlic, salt, bay leaf, remaining herbs (crushed fine) and sesame seeds; bring to a boil. Pour over vegetables and cover tightly (use a layer of foil before putting on cover). Bake for 60–75 minutes, gently mixing twice during cooking. Uncover and sprinkle generously with Parmesan and cover with thinly sliced Monterey Jack cheese. Place under broiler until cheese is bubbly and golden. *Variation:* Instead of rosemary, chili, and thyme, use 1/2 teaspoon each of savory and tarragon. *Suggestion:* Serve with thickly sliced bread.

Ingredients continued

½ cup grated Parmesan cheese

⅓ pound Monterey Jack cheese

Nutritional Analysis *for 1 serving {377 g}*

Calories 348   Calories from fat 206

Nutrient: % Calories from:		Nutrient: % Calories from:	
Total fat 23 g	57 %	Total carbohydrate 24 g	27 %
Saturated fat 8 g	20 %	Dietary fiber 6 g	
Cholesterol 29 mg		Sugars 8 g	
Sodium 1,065 mg		Protein 15 g	16 %

% Daily:

Vitamin A, 115 %; Vitamin C, 151 %; Calcium, 38 %; Iron, 14 %

WILL HUTCHINS

WILL HUTCHINS
☆ Corn Pudding

I am not a devout vegetarian, but I'm a devout believer in vegetarianism. Years ago I discovered that the less meat I ate, the more energy I had in my acting. Vegetables equal life force.

4 Servings

¼ cup onions, chopped

2 tablespoons all-purpose flour

2 tablespoons butter

1 cup milk

1 cup corn (canned, frozen or kernels from 2 ears of fresh corn

1½ teaspoons salt

¼ teaspoon black pepper

1½ teaspoons sugar

2 eggs, beaten

1 cup fresh raspberries

Preheat oven to 350°F. Sauté onion in 1 tablespoon butter and set aside. Melt remaining butter in saucepan and stir in flour. Pour milk in slowly, stirring until smooth. Bring to boil, add corn, sautéed onion, sugar, beaten eggs, salt, and pepper. Mix well. Pour into buttered 7-inch baking dish. Bake for 35–40 minutes, until lightly browned. Serve for dessert with fresh raspberries. "This is my favorite dish besides my wife."

Nutritional Analysis for 1 serving {180 g}
Calories 206   Calories from fat 99

Nutrient:	% Calories from:	Nutrient:	% Calories from:
Total fat 11 g	46 %	Total carbohydrate 22 g	41 %
Saturated fat 6 g	24 %	Dietary fiber 3 g	
Cholesterol 130 mg		Sugars 9 g	
Sodium 926 mg		Protein 7 g	14 %

% Daily:
Vitamin A, 14 %; Vitamin C, 19 %; Calcium, 10 %; Iron, 6 %

ANNE JEFFREYS

ANNE JEFFREYS

☆ Thomas Jefferson's Chess Pie

8 Servings

¼ cup butter

½ cup sugar

1 cup dark brown sugar

⅛ teaspoon salt

3 eggs

1 teaspoon vanilla

2 tablespoons all-purpose flour

½ cup heavy cream

1 cup chopped pecans

1 unbaked piecrust

1 teaspoon apricot brandy

2 teaspoons apricot preserves

While I eat mostly vegetables and fruits, I do indulge in chicken and fish occasionally—and even vegetarians like sweets!—but I never eat red meat, veal, or lamb.

Preheat oven to 375°F. Cream butter, add sugars and salt; cream thoroughly. Add eggs one at a time, beating well after each addition. Stir in vanilla, flour, cream, and pecans. For glaze, blend brandy and preserves until liquefied. Paint the piecrust with apricot glaze. Spoon in filling and bake 40–50 minutes or until knife inserted halfway between edge and middle of filling comes out clean. Don't overbake. *Suggestion:* Garnish with tiny baked pastry leaves.

Nutritional Analysis   *for 1 serving {124 g}*

Calories 484   Calories from fat 271

Nutrient:	% Calories from:	Nutrient:	% Calories from:
Total fat 30 g	54 %	Total carbohydrate 53 g	42 %
Saturated fat 7 g	12 %	Dietary fiber 0 g	
Cholesterol 116 mg		Sugars 12 g	
Sodium 235 mg		Protein 6 g	4 %

% Daily:

Vitamin A, 9 %; Vitamin C, 0 %; Calcium, 4 %; Iron, 7 %

Best Regards
James Earl Jones

JAMES EARL JONES

JAMES EARL JONES
☆ Fettuccine Alfredo

6 Servings

¾ *pound uncooked fettuccine*

6 tablespoons salted butter

⅔ *cup whipping cream*

½ *teaspoon salt*

⅛ *teaspoon* white pepper
(large pinch)*

⅛ *teaspoon* ground nutmeg
(large pinch)*

*1 cup grated Parmesan
cheese*

Cook fettuccine in salted water 6–8 minutes, drain, and return it to dry pot. While fettuccine is cooking, place butter and cream in heavy skillet over medium heat. Cook, stirring, for 2 minutes, until well blended and bubbling. Stir in salt, pepper, and nutmeg; remove from heat. Gradually add Parmesan cheese until well blended. Return to heat if necessary to melt cheese. Pour sauce over fettuccine. Toss with form until well coated. Serve immediately. *Variation:* Cook 1 or 2 dozen sliced mushroom caps in butter before adding milk or cream to be added to sauce/pasta.

Nutritional Analysis   *for 1 serving {115 g}*

Calories 429   Calories from fat 255

Nutrient: % Calories from:		Nutrient: % Calories from:	
Total fat 28 g	59 %	Total carbohydrate 31 g	29 %
Saturated fat 17 g	34 %	Dietary fiber 0 g	
Cholesterol 91 mg		Sugars 1 g	
Sodium 625 mg		Protein 14 g	13 %

% Daily:

Vitamin A, 26 %; Vitamin C, 0 %; Calcium, 25 %; Iron, 5 %

SHIRLEY JONES AND MARTY INGELS

SHIRLEY JONES AND MARTY INGELS
☆ Marty's Nutty Cheese Roll

16 Servings

8 ounces cream cheese

2 ounces blue cheese, crumbled fine

4 ounces shredded Cheddar cheese

¼ teaspoon garlic powder

1 tablespoon brandy

1 tablespoon sherry

½ teaspoon* Worcestershire sauce (dash)

⅛ teaspoon* white pepper (dash)

1 cup chopped walnuts

Blend all ingredients except nuts. Form into a ball and roll in the chopped nuts. Cover with plastic wrap and refrigerate at least 2 hours before serving.

Nutritional Analysis *for 1 serving {41 g}*
Calories 184   Calories from fat 144

Nutrient:	*% Calories from:*	*Nutrient:*	*% Calories from:*
Total fat 16 g	78 %	Total carbohydrate 4 g	8 %
Saturated fat 6 g	29 %	Dietary fiber 1 g	
Cholesterol 26 mg		Sugars 1 g	
Sodium 139 mg		Protein 6 g	12 %

% Daily:
Vitamin A, 9 %; Vitamin C, 3 %; Calcium, 10 %; Iron, 4 %

JOANNA KERNS

JOANNA KERNS
☆ My Brother's Salsa

12 Servings

1 pound canned peeled tomatoes, with liquid

¼ teaspoon salt

Juice from half a lime

1 garlic clove, crushed

1 teaspoon* olive oil

3 jalapeño peppers,* or to
taste

1 ripe avocado (8 ounces*)

1 bunch cilantro (2 ounces*)

1 bunch scallions (4 ounces*)

In a blender, add tomatoes with liquid, salt, lime juice, and garlic. In a pan, heat oil and blacken skins of from 1 to 5 jalapeños (depending on hotness desired). Put some water in a plastic bag, then empty—to dampen the sides of the bag. Place the blackened peppers in the bag and put it in the freezer for 5–10 minutes. Remove bag from the freezer and pull the skins from the jalapeños. Add the skinless peppers to blender and blend. Chop cilantro and scallions; dice avocado. Place these three ingredients in a bowl and toss. Pour blended ingredients into bowl and stir. Enjoy! *Suggestions:* Serve as a condiment with tortilla chips or over any Mexican-style dinner. *Tip:* When handling jalapeños, wear rubber gloves and avoid touching face and eyes.

Nutritional Analysis *for 1 serving {98 g}*

Calories 43   Calories from fat 28

Nutrient:	*% Calories from:*	*Nutrient:*	*% Calories from:*
Total fat 3 g	60 %	Total carbohydrate 4 g	32 %
Saturated fat 0 g	1 %	Dietary fiber 2 g	
Cholesterol 0 mg		Sugars 1 g	
Sodium 213 mg		Protein 1 g	8 %

% Daily:

Vitamin A, 4 %; Vitamin C, 18 %; Calcium, 3 %; Iron, 4 %

DEBORAH KERR

DEBORAH KERR
☆ Beetroot Cream Soup

6 Servings

1 beetroot (4 ounces*)
½ celery stalk
1 ounce salted butter
⅓ cup all-purpose flour
2 cups vegetable stock
1 teaspoon* salt
½ teaspoon* black pepper
¼ cup heavy cream

I am almost a vegetarian, but I have a husband who is a super cook, so I have to go off the rails now and then! For a healthy life and growth, people should have an adequate supply of proteins, fats, carbohydrates, mineral water, and vitamins in their diets—and there are plenty of vegetarian recipes that include these important and necessary items to keep healthy!

Peel, precook, and grate beetroot. Wash, trim, and grate celery. Melt butter in a saucepan, stir in flour, and cook without browning a few minutes. Add vegetable stock, stirring until it boils. Add beetroot and celery to stock and simmer, covered, for 30 minutes, not more, or the color will be spoiled. Pass soup through a sieve, pressing through enough beetroot to give a good color and consistency. Season carefully to taste and add cream. Heat thoroughly but without letting it boil; otherwise soup will curdle. Serve hot. *Variation:* Replace vegetable stock with milk and water.

Nutritional Analysis *for 1 serving {127 g}*
Calories 109   Calories from fat 73

Nutrient: % Calories from:		Nutrient: % Calories from:	
Total fat 8 g	67 %	Total carbohydrate 7 g	27 %
Saturated fat 2 g	20 %	Dietary fiber 0 g	
Cholesterol 24 mg		Sugars 0 g	
Sodium 768 mg		Protein 2 g	6 %

% Daily:
Vitamin A, 4 %; Vitamin C, 6 %; Calcium, 2 %; Iron, 4 %

DEBORAH KERR

☆ Vegetable Pie

4 Servings

1 ½ cups onions

2 carrots

2 celery stalks

½ cup* mushrooms ("a few")

2 teaspoons flour

1 teaspoon salt

½ teaspoon black pepper

½ cup fresh green peas

1 ounce sago or tapioca

2 ounces butter

1 short crust pastry (made using 6 ounces* whole-wheat flour)

Preheat oven to 375°F. Mince onions, carrots, celery, and mushrooms. Dust with flour seasoned with salt and pepper. Put into a pan with the peas, sago or tapioca, and very little water. Stew until three-quarters cooked. Transfer to a pie dish. Dot with little dabs of butter and cover with piecrust. Bake for 30 minutes or until golden. Allow to cool somewhat before serving. *Variation:* Pie can be made with almost any of your favorite vegetables in season.

Nutritional Analysis   ***for 1 serving {219 g}***

Calories 428   Calories from fat 246

Nutrient:	*% Calories from:*	*Nutrient:*	*% Calories from:*
Total fat 27 g	56 %	Total carbohydrate 42 g	38 %
Saturated fat 11 g	23 %	Dietary fiber 4 g	
Cholesterol 31 mg		Sugars 5 g	
Sodium 966 mg		Protein 6 g	5 %

% Daily:

Vitamin A, 113 %; Vitamin C, 27 %; Calcium, 5 %; Iron, 12 %

DEBORAH KERR
☆ Walnut Trifle

4 Servings

12 ounces custard

6 ounces stale cake crumbs

4 ounces walnuts

2 ripe bananas

¼ cup all-fruit raspberry jam

¼ cup cherries, packed in extra-heavy syrup

1 tablespoon Angelica dessert wine

Prepare custard and refrigerate until ready to use. Reserve a few whole nuts for decoration and pass remainder through a mill or chop fine. Slice the bananas. Mix the cake crumbs, bananas, and most of the chopped nuts with the jam and sufficient custard to make a fairly firm paste. Place in a dish, cover with remaining custard, and scatter remaining nut pieces on top. Decorate with whole nuts, cherries, and a drizzle of Angelica or other liqueur.

Nutritional Analysis   for 1 serving {313 g}

Calories 610   Calories from fat 245

Nutrient:	% Calories from:	Nutrient:	% Calories from:
Total fat 27 g	40 %	Total carbohydrate 78 g	51 %
Saturated fat 6 g	8 %	Dietary fiber 5 g	
Cholesterol 105 mg		Sugars 15 g	
Sodium 271 mg		Protein 13 g	8 %

% Daily:

Vitamin A, 8 %; Vitamin C, 20 %; Calcium, 18 %; Iron, 11 %

K. D. LANG

✩ Indonesian Salad With Spicy Peanut Dressing

6 Servings

2 small potatoes (6 ounces* each)

1 pound firm tofu

3 tablespoons vegetable oil

¼ teaspoon salt

½ pound spinach

Half of a small cabbage about 1 pound*

½ pound mung beans

Dressing

4 garlic cloves

¼ cup roasted peanuts

5 teaspoons soy sauce or tamari

1 ½ tablespoons each of lemon and lime juice

4 teaspoons brown sugar

¼ teaspoon cayenne pepper

2 tablespoons water

I grew up in cattle country—that's why I became a vegetarian. Meat stinks—for the animals, the environment, and your health.

The best of the East comes west in this exciting main-dish salad. Boil or steam potatoes. *Gently* press excess water out of firm tofu and cut into 1/4-inch cubes. Heat oil and salt in medium skillet over medium heat. Add the tofu in small batches and sauté until lightly browned, about 5 minutes. Remove with slotted spoon and drain on paper towels. Cut boiled or steamed potatoes into bite-size wedges. Wash spinach, cabbage, and mung beans. Steam and chop spinach; shred and lightly steam cabbage. Arrange tofu, potatoes, spinach, and cabbage on individual plates. To prepare dressing, put garlic, peanuts, soy or tamari sauce, lemon juice, lime juice, brown sugar, cayenne pepper, and water in a blender and process until smooth. If it is too thick, add another teaspoon of water. Top salad with bean sprouts and dressing, and serve immediately.

Nutritional Analysis   *for 1 serving {319 g}*

Calories 311   Calories from fat 151

Nutrient:	% Calories from:	Nutrient:	% Calories from:
Total fat 17 g	45 %	Total carbohydrate 28 g	33 %
Saturated fat 5 g	14 %	Dietary fiber 5 g	
Cholesterol 0 mg		Sugars 5 g	
Sodium 431 mg		Protein 18 g	22 %

% Daily:

Vitamin A, 28 %; Vitamin C, 100 %; Calcium, 25 %; Iron, 58 %

ROBIN LEACH

ROBIN LEACH

☆ Cassis Caviar

12 Servings

1 8-ounce* bunch fresh spinach

1 medium eggplant (2 cups*)

½ teaspoon* salt

¼ teaspoon* white pepper

2 large onions (2 cups*)

2 tablespoons vegetable oil

1 tablespoon butter

2 fresh tomatoes, sliced

12 ounces Contadina* pesto sauce

2 prepared piecrusts

6 tablespoons American caviar

Preheat oven to 400°F. Clean and steam spinach. Peel and slice eggplant thin, season to taste with salt and pepper. Sauté onions in oil until clear. Butter a shallow casserole or pie dish. Alternate layers of eggplant, onions, spinach, tomatoes, and pesto sauce. Repeat layers to top. Roll pastry to 1/8 inch thick and place on top of vegetables. Bake 20–25 minutes, or until golden. Cut into individual pieces. Garnish each piece with a dab of caviar. *Suggestion:* For special occasions, bake in individual soufflé molds.

Nutritional Analysis *for 1 serving {141 g}*

Calories 327   Calories from fat 237

Nutrient:	% Calories from:	Nutrient:	% Calories from:
Total fat 26 g	71 %	Total carbohydrate 17 g	21 %
Saturated fat 3 g	9 %	Dietary fiber 2 g	
Cholesterol 54 mg		Sugars 1 g	
Sodium 560 mg		Protein 7 g	8 %

% Daily:

Vitamin A, 17 %; Vitamin C, 17 %; Calcium, 5 %; Iron, 16 %

ART LINKLETTER

ART LINKLETTER

★ # Minestrone

12 Servings

One of my favorite all-time soups.

½ cup olive oil

6 garlic cloves, peeled and chopped

2 large Spanish onions, diced

6 carrots, scraped and diced

3 large celery stalks, sliced

1 ½ teaspoons salt

1 medium head cabbage (2 pounds*), shredded

10 large leaves of kale (2 ounces*), chopped

½ teaspoon thyme

2 bay leaves, broken

3 quarts water

1 28-ounce can plum tomatoes

1 pound chickpeas, cooked

1 cup small pasta, penne, or small shells

½ teaspoon* black pepper

½ teaspoon* salt

Heat olive oil in a 10-quart pot. Add garlic, onions, carrots, celery, and 1/2 teaspoon of the salt and sauté over low heat until onions are wilted but not brown. Add cabbage, kale, thyme, bay leaves, and remaining teaspoon of salt. Increase heat, stirring constantly for about 1 minute; then add water, tomatoes, and chickpeas, and bring to a full boil. Lower heat and simmer, covered, for 45 minutes. Add the pasta and cook for an additional 15 minutes, or until pasta is tender. Season with salt and pepper to taste. Serve with good bread and butter or garlic oil.

Note: This soup freezes well.

Nutritional Analysis   *for 1 serving {529 g}*

Calories 260   Calories from fat 117

Nutrient:	% Calories from:	Nutrient:	% Calories from:
Total fat 13 g	43 %	Total carbohydrate 31 g	46 %
Saturated fat 2 g	7 %	Dietary fiber 6 g	
Cholesterol 3 mg		Sugars 8 g	
Sodium 642 mg		Protein 8 g	11 %

% Daily:

Vitamin A, 105 %; Vitamin C, 84 %; Calcium, 10 %; Iron, 13 %

RUE McCLANAHAN

RUE MCCLANAHAN
Sweet and Sour Peppers

2 Servings

5 bell peppers: a combination of red, green, and yellow; stemmed, cored, seeded, and sliced

3 ounces red onion, minced

1 teaspoon basil

⅔ cup pineapple juice

⅓ cup balsamic vinegar

1 tablespoon arrowroot

Compassion is the foundation of everything positive, everything good. If you carry the power of compassion to the marketplace and the dinner table, you can make your life really count.

Toss peppers and minced onions together (use a combination of red, green, and yellow peppers) and set aside. Whisk other ingredients together over a moderate flame in a saucepan. Stir until sauce thickens. Steam peppers for 2 minutes and toss with sauce. May be served immediately or chilled and served cold. *Suggestions:* Serve with Lynda Day-George's Potatoes Lynda or over Willard Scott's Baked Rice.

Nutritional Analysis   *for 1 serving {599 g}*
Calories 181   Calories from fat 5

Nutrient: % Calories from:	Nutrient: % Calories from:
Total fat 1 g 3 %	Total carbohydrate 42 g 87 %
Saturated fat 0 g 0 %	Dietary fiber 7 g
Cholesterol 0 mg	Sugars 23 g
Sodium 18 mg	Protein 5 g 10 %

% Daily:
Vitamin A, 12 %; Vitamin C, 571 %; Calcium, 6 %; Iron, 28 %

HAYLEY MILLS

☆ Pasta With Fresh Tomatoes

8 Servings

1 cup olive oil

3 garlic cloves, peeled and minced

1 cup basil leaves, washed and cut in strips

2 ½ teaspoons salt

½ teaspoon black pepper

4 tomatoes, cubed

16 ounces brie cheese, rind off, cubed

24 ounces linguine, white and green mixed

1 teaspoon olive oil

8 tablespoons freshly grated Parmesan cheese

Unbelievable! Goes great with salad and crusty French bread. Mamma mia!!

Pour olive oil into mixing bowl and stir in garlic, basil, salt, and pepper. Add tomatoes and brie; coat thoroughly and allow to marinate at least 2 1/2 hours. At mealtime, drop linguine in rapidly boiling water with 1 teaspoon olive oil. Drain and mix with tomatoe-brie elixir: brie should melt. Sprinkle with fresh Parmesan and serve immediately.

Nutritional Analysis   *for 1 serving {245 g}*

Calories 791   Calories from fat 420

Nutrient: % Calories from:		Nutrient: % Calories from:	
Total fat 47 g	53 %	Total carbohydrate 68 g	34 %
Saturated fat 15 g	17 %	Dietary fiber 1 g	
Cholesterol 61 mg		Sugars 2 g	
Sodium 1,150 mg		Protein 26 g	13 %

% Daily:

Vitamin A, 16 %; Vitamin C, 20 %; Calcium, 22 %; Iron, 23 %

JULIE NEWMAR

JULIE NEWMAR
☆ Eggplant Sauce With Pasta

8 Servings

6 garlic cloves, crushed

½ cup olive oil

18 ounces (3 small cans) tomato paste

2 medium eggplants (about 1 pound each)

2 small red bell peppers, seeded and diced

3 cups peeled and chopped tomatoes

1 15-ounce can black olives, chopped

1 tablespoon oregano

½ teaspoon basil

¼ teaspoon red pepper flakes

2 cups red wine

2 tablespoons sugar

½ teaspoon* salt

24 ounces pasta such as mafalda or rotini

In a skillet sauté garlic in oil until golden. Add tomato paste and cook over medium heat about 20 minutes, or until very dark, stirring often from the bottom. Meanwhile, wash eggplants and chop into 1/2-inch cubes. When tomato paste is a rich, dark color, add peppers, eggplant, tomatoes, and olives, stirring to coat evenly. Stir in remaining ingredients (except pasta), cover and simmer on medium-low heat for about an hour, stirring occasionally and scraping the bottom to prevent scorching. Add water or extra wine if sauce gets too thick. Serve over fresh-cooked pasta.

Nutritional Analysis *for 1 serving {513 g}*

Calories 488   Calories from fat 246

Nutrient:	% Calories from:	Nutrient:	% Calories from:
Total fat 27 g	45 %	Total carbohydrate 53 g	39 %
Saturated fat 3 g	5 %	Dietary fiber 6 g	
Cholesterol 28 mg		Sugars 7 g	
Sodium 1,170 mg		Protein 11 g	8 %

% Daily:

Vitamin A, 25 %; Vitamin C, 69 %; Calcium, 13 %; Iron, 27 %

☆ Pasta With Tomato Sauce

4 Servings

½ teaspoon* salt

1 pound* fresh pasta

½ medium onion, minced

3 tablespoons virgin olive oil

28 ounces* canned plum tomatoes, chopped

¼ teaspoon* red pepper (optional)

1 cup* fresh peeled plum tomatoes, chopped

4 tablespoons* grated Parmesan cheese

1 teaspoon* freshly milled black pepper

8 whole basil leaves*

"I cook [this] for my three children. . . . They love it! Bon appétit!"

Put salted water on to boil over high heat and add pasta when boiling. Meanwhile, sauté onion in 2 tablespoons of the oil until clear and golden. Add canned plum tomatoes and red pepper, and simmer for 5 minutes. Add fresh tomatoes, stir, and simmer an additional 15 minutes. When pasta is al dente, drain and transfer to a bowl. Toss with remaining tablespoon of the olive oil. Ladle on tomato sauce, add freshly grated Parmesan and black pepper, and garnish with fresh basil leaves.

Nutritional Analysis *for 1 serving {410 g}*

Calories 330   Calories from fat 126

Nutrient:	*% Calories from:*	*Nutrient:*	*% Calories from:*
Total fat 14 g	37 %	Total carbohydrate 42 g	50 %
Saturated fat 3 g	8 %	Dietary fiber 2 g	
Cholesterol 43 mg		Sugars 2 g	
Sodium 717 mg		Protein 11 g	13 %

% Daily:

Vitamin A, 6 %; Vitamin C, 21 %; Calcium, 11 %; Iron, 17 %

GREGORY PECK

GREGORY PECK

☆ Ratatouille

4 Servings

4 bell peppers
2 large onions
4 tomatoes
1 ½ pounds eggplant
1 pound zucchini
4 tablespoons olive oil
1 teaspoon salt
1 teaspoon black pepper
2 tablespoons fines herbes
(mixed herbs)

Trim stems from peppers, remove seeds and membrane, and cut into julienne strips. Peel and chop onions, tomatoes, eggplant, and zucchini. Heat oil over medium-high heat in a casserole. Add onions and cook them gently until they are very soft, stirring often so they do not brown. Add chopped tomatoes, eggplant, and zucchini to onions, season to taste with salt and pepper, and cook over low heat for 30 minutes, stirring occasionally. When veggies are tender, let cool slightly and sprinkle with fines herbes. Serve warm or at room temperature.

Nutritional Analysis *for 1 serving {585 g}*
Calories 273   Calories from fat 135

Nutrient:	**% Calories from:**	**Nutrient:**	**% Calories from:**
Total fat 15 g	45 %	Total carbohydrate 34 g	46 %
Saturated fat 2 g	6 %	Dietary fiber 5 g	
Cholesterol 0 mg		Sugars 10 g	
Sodium 559 mg		Protein 7 g	9 %

% Daily:
Vitamin A, 21 %; Vitamin C, 181 %; Calcium, 14 %; Iron, 27 %

Best wishes

Lynn Redgrave

(PHOTOGRAPH BY MICHAEL MARON)

LYNN REDGRAVE

LYNN REDGRAVE
O'Redgrave's Irish Soda Bread

24 Servings

4 cups stone-ground whole-wheat flour

2 cups all-purpose flour

1 teaspoon baking soda

1 teaspoon salt

2 cups low-fat (1% milk fat) buttermilk

This recipe is from my book This is Living. *Because this bread uses baking soda instead of yeast as its rising agent the dough doesn't have to be given special rising time. This makes the bread quick and easy to prepare. Wrapping the hot bread in a clean cloth before it cools gives the crust a deliciously crunchy consistency.*

Preheat oven to 375°F. In large mixing bowl combine whole-wheat flour, 1 1/2 cups of the all-purpose flour, baking soda, and salt, mixing well to combine. Make a well in the center of flour mixture; pour in milk. Using a large metal spoon, mix well to combine. Using your hands, knead in bowl until well combined. Sprinkle remaining all-purpose flour onto work surface; turn dough out onto floured surface and knead until smooth, 1 or 2 minutes. Shape dough into 7-inch round loaf about 3 inches thick and transfer to nonstick baking sheet. Using a sharp knife, cut a cross about 1 inch deep through the surface of the dough. Bake for 40–45 minutes (until a toothpick inserted in center comes out dry). Transfer bread to wire rack and let cool completely. To serve, cut into 24 equal slices.

Nutritional Analysis   *for 1 serving {69 g}*

Calories 176   Calories from fat 7

Nutrient:	*% Calories from:*	*Nutrient:*	*% Calories from:*
Total fat 1 g	4 %	Total carbohydrate 36 g	81 %
Saturated fat 0 g	1 %	Dietary fiber 1 g	
Cholesterol 0 mg		Sugars 2 g	
Sodium 154 mg		Protein 6 g	15 %

% Daily:

Vitamin A, 1 %; Vitamin C, 0 %; Calcium, 4 %; Iron, 15 %

CARL REINER

CARL REINER
Estelle's Baked Beans

4 Servings

1 pound pea beans or navy beans

1 cup chopped onion

2 tablespoons packed brown sugar

½ teaspoon mustard powder

1 cup molasses or honey

1 teaspoon salt

½ teaspoon black pepper

Soak pea beans or navy beans overnight. Drain, rinse, and cook in 2 quarts water until skins start to come off. Drain and save liquid. Combine onion, brown sugar, mustard, molasses, salt, and pepper in a small bowl, mixing completely. Place beans in a 3-quart ovenproof casserole and stir in onion mixture. Add enough bean water to cover, plus 2 inches; if there's not enough bean water, use plain water, bouillon, or cider. Don't stir! Cover and bake in 300°F oven for 8 hours or in a 350°F oven for 6 hours.

Nutritional Analysis   *for 1 serving {244 g}*
Calories 319   Calories from fat 9

Nutrient:	% Calories from:	Nutrient:	% Calories from:
Total fat 1 g	3 %	Total carbohydrate 77 g	89 %
Saturated fat 0 g	0 %	Dietary fiber 1 g	
Cholesterol 0 mg		Sugars 1 g	
Sodium 550 mg		Protein 7 g	8 %

% Daily:
Vitamin A, 0 %; Vitamin C, 5 %; Calcium, 16 %; Iron, 21 %

GERALDO RIVERA

GERALDO RIVERA
Eggplant Rodriguez

4 Servings

1 medium eggplant

1 ounce tomato paste

½ cup diced onion

1 garlic clove, peeled and diced

¼ cup diced green bell pepper

1 cilantro branch

⅛ teaspoon* oregano ("pinch")

¼ teaspoon* salt ("pinch")

⅛ teaspoon* black pepper ("pinch")

1 cup water

2 cups white rice, cooked

Peel and cut eggplant into 1-inch cubes. In a saucepan mix the remaining ingredients (except the rice) with 1/4 cup of the water. Cook over low heat for about 8 minutes. Add the rest of the water and the eggplant, and cover the pan. Cook from 12–15 minutes over medium heat. Serve over rice. *Suggestion:* Great with salad and garlic bread.

Nutritional Analysis   *for 1 serving {366 g}*

Calories 186   Calories from fat 5

Nutrient:	**% Calories from:**	**Nutrient:**	**% Calories from:**
Total fat 1 g	3 %	Total carbohydrate 41 g	87 %
Saturated fat 0 g	1 %	Dietary fiber 1 g	
Cholesterol 0 mg		Sugars 1 g	
Sodium 161 mg		Protein 5 g	10 %

% Daily:

Vitamin A, 5 %; Vitamin C, 30 %; Calcium, 3 %; Iron, 13 %

GERALDO RIVERA
Green Banana Salad

6 Servings

10 green bananas
2 packets Goya Sazón Accent
1 ½ teaspoons olive oil
½ teaspoon white vinegar
1 medium onion, sliced thin
2 tablespoons capers, minced
12 strips of pimiento, minced
2 roasted red peppers,
chopped
2 bay leaves

Peel and boil green bananas until tender but not too soft. When done, place bananas in cold water to cool and cut in 1/4-inch slices. Mix all other ingredients together and toss gently with the bananas. Serve at room temperature.

Nutritional Analysis *for 1 serving {290 g}*
Calories 237   Calories from fat 46

Nutrient:	% Calories from:	Nutrient:	% Calories from:
Total fat 5 g	17 %	Total carbohydrate 51 g	77 %
Saturated fat 1 g	2 %	Dietary fiber 4 g	
Cholesterol 0 mg		Sugars 31 g	
Sodium 366 mg		Protein 3 g	5 %

% Daily:
Vitamin A, 2 %; Vitamin C, 34 %; Calcium, 2 %; Iron, 4 %

GERALDO RIVERA

☆ Hilda's Caramel Custard

8 Servings

1 cup sugar

4 large eggs, beaten slightly

1 cup water

1 14-ounce can condensed milk

1 12-ounce can evaporated milk

½ teaspoon vanilla

Prepare caramel as follows: Place sugar in fireproof bowl over medium heat. Stir until melted (do not burn) and let it cool. Mix all other ingredients well and pour over caramel. Place bowl in a double boiler and cook until knife comes out clean. Cool, then refrigerate for 2 hours before serving.

Nutritional Analysis   *for 1 serving {172 g}*

Calories 357   Calories from fat 92

Nutrient: % Calories from:		Nutrient: % Calories from:	
Total fat 10 g	26 %	Total carbohydrate 57 g	64 %
Saturated fat 3 g	7 %	Dietary fiber 0 g	
Cholesterol 141 mg		Sugars 24 g	
Sodium 134 mg		Protein 10 g	11 %

% Daily:

Vitamin A, 7 %; Vitamin C, 12 %; Calcium, 12 %; Iron, 3 %

(FAMILY COMMUNICATIONS INC. ©)

FRED ROGERS

FRED ROGERS
☆ Tofu Burgers

8 Servings

1 cup onions, minced

3 tablespoons canola oil

20 ounces firm tofu

2/3 cup breadcrumbs

3 eggs

2 tablespoons Worcestershire sauce

1 tablespoon soy sauce

½ teaspoon* garlic salt, or to taste

2 tablespoons unsalted butter

Sauté onions in oil until tender but not brown. Cool. Drain tofu and crumble into medium mixing bowl. Mix in sautéed onions, breadcrumbs, eggs, sauces, and garlic salt, combining thoroughly. Form into eight patties and fry in butter until crisp and evenly browned on both sides.

Nutritional Analysis   for 1 serving {133 g}

Calories 245   Calories from fat 150

Nutrient:	% Calories from:	Nutrient:	% Calories from:
Total fat 17 g	58 %	Total carbohydrate 12 g	19 %
Saturated fat 4 g	13 %	Dietary fiber 1 g	
Cholesterol 88 mg		Sugars 1 g	
Sodium 417 mg		Protein 15 g	23 %

% Daily:

Vitamin A, 8 %; Vitamin C, 14 %; Calcium, 17 %; Iron 46 %

PAT SAJAK

PAT SAJAK
☆ Gin Fizz Egg Pie

8 Servings

6 Morningstar* meatless
bacon strips

3 servings Cooking spray
(3 seconds of spray)

1 cup chopped onion

1 tablespoon Heart Beat*
canola oil

1 28-ounce can whole peeled
tomatoes

1 cup mushrooms, sliced

1 package Lightlife* Tofu
Pups, sliced ¼ inch thick

6 ounces Monterey Jack
cheese, shredded

12 eggs

½ cup cream

1 shaker of gin fizzes**

2 ounces* grated Parmesan
cheese

8 thin pimiento strips

8 tablespoons sour cream

Prepare meatless "bacon" strips according to manufacturer's instructions until just starting to darken. Cool and crumble into small pieces. Preheat oven to 350°F. Coat casserole dish with cooking spray. Sauté onion in oil until beginning to brown. Stir in tomatoes, mushrooms, and cocktail-frank slices; simmer about 15 minutes. During the last minutes, stir in Jack cheese, reserving 2 tablespoons for the top. Gently beat eggs with cream. Combine with pan mixture. Bake 30 minutes; remove from oven and sprinkle Parmesan and reserved Jack cheese over top and return to oven for 15 minutes, or until pie has a nice golden crust. Allow to cool somewhat before cutting. *Suggestions*: Make a shaker of gin fizzes on entry of pan to oven and enjoy, enjoy until eggs are done. Serve pie in slices, garnished with thin strips of pimiento and small dollops of sour cream.

Nutritional Analysis   *for 1 serving {313 g}*
Calories 491   Calories from fat 293

Nutrient: % Calories from:	Nutrient: % Calories from:
Total fat 33 g 64 %	Total carbohydrate 11 g 10 %
Saturated fat 14 g 27 %	Dietary fiber 1 g
Cholesterol 371 mg	Sugars 4 g
Sodium 592 mg	Protein 30 g 26 %

% Daily:
Vitamin A, 42 %; Vitamin C, 28 %; Calcium, 36 %; Iron, 11 %

WILLARD SCOTT

WILLARD SCOTT
☆ Baked Rice

4 Servings

1 stick (4 ounces) butter or margarine

1 large onion, peeled and diced

2 10-ounce cans consommé

1 cup uncooked rice

Preheat oven to 350°F. Butter casserole dish with a little of the butter. Melt remaining butter or margarine in medium skillet and sauté onions until tender and golden. Add consommé and rice. Stir and transfer to buttered casserole dish. Bake covered for 1 hour. Remove from oven and serve directly from casserole dish. *Variation*: About 20 minutes before baking time is up, pour in a small can of drained mushrooms (buttons or pieces). "Ummmm, delicious!"

Nutritional Analysis   *for 1 serving {256 g}*

Calories 418   Calories from fat 211

Nutrient:	*% Calories from:*	*Nutrient:*	*% Calories from:*
Total fat 23 g	50 %	Total carbohydrate 43 g	41 %
Saturated fat 14 g	31 %	Dietary fiber 1 g	
Cholesterol 62 mg		Sugars 1 g	
Sodium 1,177 mg		Protein 9 g	9 %

% Daily:

Vitamin A, 21 %; Vitamin C, 4 %; Calcium, 3 %; Iron, 14 %   115

BROOKE SHIELDS

BROOKE SHIELDS
Vegetable Health Soup

5 Servings

2 Granny Smith apples, peeled and chopped

1 large onion, peeled and chopped

2 servings cooking spray (2 seconds of spray)

2 large sprinkles Mrs. Dash seasoning (½ teaspoon*)

1 large bunch (1½ pounds*) broccoli, cauliflower, or carrots**

1 46-ounce can Swansons* vegetable broth

**Use any one vegetable; broccoli was used for Nutritional Analysis.

Sauté apples and onion sprinkled with Mrs. Dash in a nonstick frying pan lightly coated with cooking spray. Set aside. Clean, scrub, and chop the vegetable, including stalks, into 1-inch pieces. Steam or parboil. Add all ingredients to broth and simmer for 10 minutes. Pour into blender and purée.

Suggestions: May be served cold with a dab of low-fat cottage cheese in the center. Garnish with parsley in winter, mint in summer.

Nutritional Analysis   for 1 serving {481 g}
Calories 108   Calories from fat 21

Nutrient:	*% Calories from:*	*Nutrient:*	*% Calories from:*
Total fat 2 g	19 %	Total carbohydrate 18 g	65 %
Saturated fat 0 g	1 %	Dietary fiber 6 g	
Cholesterol 0 mg		Sugars 10 g	
Sodium 1,205 mg		Protein 5 g	16 %

% Daily:
Vitamin A, 21 %; Vitamin C, 218 %; Calcium, 7 %; Iron, 7 %

With much love,
Elizabeth Taylor

(PHOTOGRAPHER: BRUCE WEBER 1991)

ELIZABETH TAYLOR

ELIZABETH TAYLOR
Low-Cal Vinaigrette

4 Servings

1 garlic clove, crushed

5 tablespoons stock or bouillon

1 tablespoon vegetable oil

1 tablespoon lemon juice

1 tablespoon balsamic or other vinegar

½ tablespoon chives

½ teaspoon chervil

⅛ teaspoon* Tabasco sauce, or less, to taste

¼ teaspoon* salt

¼ teaspoon* black pepper

Combine first seven ingredients and set aside to marinate at least 2 hours. Add Tabasco, salt, and pepper to taste. Stir briskly to mix before serving. *Suggestions:* Great over salads, as a dip for crudités, or as a dressing for cooked vegetables.

Nutritional Analysis *for 1 serving {31 g}*

Calories 37   Calories from fat 31

Nutrient:	% Calories from:	Nutrient:	% Calories from:
Total fat 3 g	82 %	Total carbohydrate 2 g	17 %
Saturated fat 2 g	43 %	Dietary fiber 0 g	
Cholesterol 0 mg		Sugars 0 g	
Sodium 214 mg		Protein 0 g	1 %

% Daily:

Vitamin A, 0 %; Vitamin C, 2 %; Calcium, 0 %; Iron, 1 %

DANIEL J. TRAVANTI

DANIEL J. TRAVANTI
Fat-Free Oat Bran Muffins

12 Muffins

2 ¼ cups Trader Joe's* oat bran

1 tablespoon baking powder

½ cups raisins

1 teaspoon cinnamon

1¼ cups apple juice

1 cup apples, finely diced, peeled or unpeeled

2 egg whites (or egg substitute), beaten frothy

Preheat oven to 425°F. In a bowl combine first four ingredients; add apple juice and apples. Fold in eggs and mix thoroughly. Bake in ungreased muffin tins for 13 minutes. *Note:* "These muffins contain no refined sugar, no flour, and, because they are oil-free, they are practically fat-free!"

Nutritional Analysis *for 1 serving {73 g}*

Calories 88   Calories from fat 12

Nutrient:	% Calories from:	Nutrient:	% Calories from:
Total fat 1 g	10 %	Total carbohydrate 23 g	76 %
Saturated fat 0 g	2 %	Dietary fiber 3 g	
Cholesterol 0 mg		Sugars 9 g	
Sodium 16 mg		Protein 4 g	13 %

% Daily:

Vitamin A, 0 %; Vitamin C, 20 %; Calcium, 3 %; Iron, 7 %

JOAN VAN ARK

Joan's Hummus

8 Servings

2 tablespoons parsley
⅓ cup tahini
⅓ cup lemon juice
¼ cup water
2 tablespoons olive oil
2 garlic cloves, peeled
2 cups cooked chickpeas

Put all ingredients except chickpeas into a food processor or blender and blend until garlic is smooth. Add chickpeas and blend until smooth or to desired texture. Serve and enjoy! *Suggestions:* Enjoy with falafel, pita bread, crackers, pretzels, grated carrots, onions, or tomatoes. Keeps in fridge about two weeks. Tastes great!

Nutritional Analysis   *for 1 serving {39 g}*
Calories 100   Calories from fat 80

Nutrient:	% Calories from:	Nutrient:	% Calories from:
Total fat 9 g	75 %	Total carbohydrate 4 g	17 %
Saturated fat 1 g	11 %	Dietary fiber 1 g	
Cholesterol 0 mg		Sugars 0 g	
Sodium 18 mg		Protein 2 g	8 %

% Daily:
Vitamin A, 2 %; Vitamin C, 17 %; Calcium, 2 %; Iron, 4 %

☆ Pasta With Pesto Sauce and Broccoli

4 Servings

1 pound fresh pasta such as fettucine and angel hair
2 garlic cloves, peeled
¼ cup grated Parmesan
¼ cup pine nuts
1 stalk broccoli, steamed
1 teaspoon crushed red pepper
½ teaspoon* black pepper
½ teaspoon* salt
¼ cup olive oil

Cook pasta in boiling water. Meanwhile, put remaining ingredients except oil into blender or food processor and blend thoroughly. While machine is running, add olive oil slowly until blended. Serve with cooked pasta and enjoy!

Nutritional Analysis   *for 1 serving {200 g}*
Calories 357   Calories from fat 183

Nutrient:	% Calories from:	Nutrient:	% Calories from:
Total fat 20 g	51 %	Total carbohydrate 33 g	37 %
Saturated fat 4 g	10 %	Dietary fiber 4 g	
Cholesterol 43 mg		Sugars 1 g	
Sodium 414 mg		Protein 11 g	13 %

% Daily:
Vitamin A, 5 %; Vitamin C, 86 %; Calcium, 12 %; Iron, 11 %

BARBARA WALTERS

BARBARA WALTERS
☆ Roasted Eggplant Soup

6 Servings

1 ½ pounds shiny eggplants, washed and halved

1 large red onion

1 large red bell pepper

2 medium-size ripe tomatoes

6 tablespoons olive oil

2 garlic cloves, peeled and chopped

½ teaspoon dried thyme or 4 or 5 branches of fresh thyme

1 bay leaf

1 teaspoon dried basil

1 teaspoon salt

2 tablespoons fresh basil, chopped (optional)

7 cups water (or stock)

2 tablespoons lemon juice

Preheat oven to 400°F. Brush eggplants, onion, pepper, and tomatoes with 4 tablespoons of the olive oil, pricking eggplants so oil sinks in. Bake eggplants for 20 minutes, then add onion, pepper, and tomatoes. Cook until eggplant is soft and beginning to collapse, and the skins of all the vegetables are loose, wrinkled, and blackened. Remove from oven and cool briefly. Remove all skins, seed the pepper, and roughly chop all vegetables. Slowly warm the remaining olive oil with the garlic and dried herbs. After several minutes add the baked vegetables, salt, and chopped fresh basil. Pour in the water or stock and bring to a boil. Cover and simmer for 25 minutes. Cool the soup briefly, then purée in a blender at low speed, preserving some texture. Return soup to the pot and season to taste with salt and lemon juice. Thin with additional water or stock, if needed. *Note:* If the soup stands for very long before serving, it may be necessary to thin it further.

Nutritional Analysis   *for 1 serving {570 g}*
Calories 198   Calories from fat 127

Nutrient:	% Calories from:	Nutrient:	% Calories from:
Total fat 14 g	60 %	Total carbohydrate 18 g	34 %
Saturated fat 2 g	8 %	Dietary fiber 1 g	
Cholesterol 0 mg		Sugars 4 g	
Sodium 377 mg		Protein 3 g	5 %

% Daily:
Vitamin A, 5 %; Vitamin C, 28 %; Calcium, 4 %; Iron, 12 %

(PHOTOGRAPH BY ALICE BILLINGS)

DENNIS WEAVER

DENNIS WEAVER

☆ Dennis and Gerry's Vegetable Soup

6 Servings

1 medium onion, chopped

6 celery stalks, chopped

2 carrots, chopped

⅓ cup canola oil

8 ounces (or more) tomato juice

5 ripe tomatoes, blended

2 cups bottled water

1 small zucchini, chopped

1 cup cooked brown rice

½ cup shredded cabbage

3 sprigs watercress

3 tablespoons soy sauce, miso, or liquid amino acids

½ teaspoon* fines herbes (assorted herbs to taste) or to taste

Sauté chopped onion, celery, and carrots in oil until medium cooked, about 10 minutes. Add tomato juice, blended tomatoes, and water. Add chopped zucchini, cooked rice, cabbage, watercress, soy sauce, and herbs. Cook until tender: about 5 minutes. Vegetables should still be firm. Serve immediately. *Variations:* Instead of brown rice, add quinoa, cooked soybeans, wheat kernels, or chickpeas. Try miso or liquid amino acids in place of soy sauce. *Suggestion:* Top with butter or fat-free margarine.

Nutritional Analysis   *for 1 serving {415 g}*

Calories 212   Calories from fat 119

Nutrient: % Calories from:		Nutrient: % Calories from:	
Total fat 13 g	53 %	Total carbohydrate 23 g	40 %
Saturated fat 1 g	4 %	Dietary fiber 4 g	
Cholesterol 0 mg		Sugars 8 g	
Sodium 734 mg		Protein 4 g	7 %

% Daily:

Vitamin A, 78 %; Vitamin C, 70 %; Calcium, 7 %; Iron, 10 %

VANNA WHITE

VANNA WHITE
☆ Cottage Cheese Salad

6 Servings

32 ounces plain cottage cheese

1 3-ounce package Jell-O

8 ounces canned crushed pineapple (with juice)

8 ounces Cool Whip whipped topping

In a bowl mix cottage cheese and any flavor of Jell-o (I use lime). Drain pineapple and add to mixture. Fold in whipped topping. Refrigerate until ready to serve. *Suggestion:* Add chopped walnuts or pecans if desired.

Nutritional Analysis *for 1 serving {241 g}*

Calories 338   Calories from fat 138

Nutrient:	% Calories from:	Nutrient:	% Calories from:
Total fat 15 g	45 %	Total carbohydrate 18 g	24 %
Saturated fat 4 g	13 %	Dietary fiber 0 g	
Cholesterol 24 mg		Sugars 13 g	
Sodium 982 mg		Protein 24 g	32 %

% Daily:

Vitamin A, 16 %; Vitamin C, 6 %; Calcium, 10 %; Iron 2 %

PART 2

CELEBRITY REDUX

In this section you can find nutritionally altered versions of many of the original celebrity recipes. I call them REDUXed recipes, playing both on the Latin word for "redo" and the word "reduce," thus these recipes are redone with an eye toward reduction. For the most part, they reflect reductions in sodium, fats, cholesterol, and calories. I have made all of these changes while remaining as true as possible to the taste, texture, and appearance of the original recipe.

As you will see, these Reduxed versions reflect substitution of ingredients and brand names, and elimination of certain ingredients, particularly salt. Compare the nutritional profile of the REDUX to the original to help you plan your nutritional intake. A reasonable objective is 20 percent fat; 65 percent carbohydrates, and 15 percent protein

Throughout this section, I have also included suggestions about eating right for good health as well as for the future of the planet. Unless directly attributed, these thoughts are my own and do not reflect the personal philosophy of the generous contributors to this volume.

GRANT ALEKSANDER
Nut Loaf

6 Servings

1 serving cooking spray (1 second of spray)

4 ounces roasted chestnuts

2 ounces dry-roasted cashews

¼ cup pine nuts

3 tablespoons brewer's yeast

1½ cups cooked brown rice

1 cup cooked wild rice

1½ cups chopped or minced onion

6 ounces Soya Kaas* soy Cheddar cheese

¼ teaspoon salt

½ teaspoon black pepper

4 Ener-G* egg substitutes

8 ounces S&W* tomato sauce

Preheat oven to 350°F.

Spray 9-inch loaf pan with cooking spray. Coarsely chop nuts together. Sprinkle on brewer's yeast. Stir in remaining ingredients (except tomato sauce), pack into prepared loaf pan and shape. Bake 50 minutes. Cool 10 minutes to set up. Serve with tomato sauce.

Nutritional Analysis for 1 serving {243 g}
Calories 337   Calories from Fat 116

Nutrient:	% Calories from:	Nutrient:	% Calories from:
Total fat 13 g	34 %	Total carbohydrate 43 g	50 %
Saturated fat 2 g	6 %	Dietary fiber 7 g	
Cholesterol 0 mg		Sugars 4 g	
Sodium 361 mg		Protein 14 g	16 %

% Daily:
Vitamin A, 4 %; Vitamin C, 25 %; Calcium, 4 %; Iron, 13 %

TIM ALLEN
Tim's Favorite Manly Man Lasagne

8 Servings

1 pound eggplant

¼ teaspoon salt

2 garlic cloves

1½ cups onions, chopped

1 bell pepper

1 ½ pounds carrots

1 ½ pounds leeks, well rinsed

4 servings Pam* olive oil cooking spray (4 seconds of spray)

1 tablespoon olive oil

32 ounces Frigo* fat-free ricotta

1 teaspoon salt

½ teaspoon black pepper

30 ounces Health Valley* tomato sauce

½ pound Health Valley* whole-wheat lasagne, uncooked weight, boiled until not quite done (it will finish while the dish bakes)

½ pound Healthy Choice* nonfat mozzarella cheese, sliced thin

½ cup Weight Watchers* fat-free Parmesan cheese

Peel and chop eggplant; sprinkle lightly with salt and "sweat" for about 20 minutes. Preheat oven to 400°F. Peel and mince garlic. Chop onion, bell pepper, carrots, and leeks. Spray a large baking dish or lasagne pan with cooking spray. Sauté chopped onion in olive oil for about 5 minutes until transparent, but not brown. Add minced garlic and the chopped vegetables. Cover and cook until tender, about 15 minutes. Mix in ricotta, salt, and pepper. Cover the bottom of the baking dish with a layer of tomato sauce. Cover with a layer of lasagne, followed by a layer of the vegetable mixture. Cover this with a layer of mozzarella slices. Repeat until all ingredients are used, finishing with a layer of sauce. Sprinkle any remaining mozzarella and the Parmesan on top. Bake 1 hour. If the lasagne is getting too brown toward the end of the time, cover the dish. Allow to set up before cutting. *Variation:* Replace eggplant with zucchini.

Nutritional Analysis   *for 1 serving {561 g}*

Calories 387   Calories from fat 32

Nutrient: % Calories from:		Nutrient: % Calories from:	
Total fat 4 g	6 %	Total carbohydrate 92 g	68 %
Saturated fat 1 g	1 %	Dietary fiber 8 g	
Cholesterol 12 mg		Sugars 11 g	
Sodium 690 mg		Protein 35 g	26 %

% Daily:

Vitamin A, 275 %; Vitamin C, 84 %; Calcium, 36 %; Iron, 31 %

RICHARD ANDERSON
Greek Pasta Salad

6 Servings

2½ pounds plum tomatoes

4 ounces Sargento* feta cheese

4 ounces Mori Nu* firm tofu, crumbled

2 tablespoons fresh basil leaves, chopped

4 garlic cloves, peeled and minced

2 ounces capers, minced

2 tablespoons olive oil

1 tablespoon balsamic vinegar

1 pound penne or similar pasta

Wash and core tomatoes, cutting off stems and removing seeds (a grapefruit knife is handy for this procedure). Dice tomatoes and put into a large mixing bowl with crumbled feta and tofu, basil, garlic, capers, and olive oil, mixing gently but thoroughly. When each ingredient is coated with olive oil, splash on the balsamic vinegar. Allow to develop at room temperature for about 20–30 minutes. Meanwhile, cook the pasta in boiling water, drain, and put back into dry cooking pot immediately. Toss the fresh sauce in with steaming pasta; cover, let stand for 3–5 minutes. "Delicious served with warm, fresh French bread or rolls. Serve and Enjoy!!!"

A sound mind in a sound body. Aerobic fitness and a balanced, very low calorie diet have been shown to increase longevity and to delay the onset of many age-related diseases, including the loss of cognitive functions. Members of cultures that base their diets on low-fat plant foods live longer and have much lower rates of heart disease, cancer, diabetes, and hypertension than do members of cultures with a meat-based diet. Eat light, live long!

Nutritional Analysis   *for 1 serving {322 g}*

Calories 415   Calories from fat 95

Nutrient:	% Calories from:	Nutrient:	% Calories from:
Total fat 11 g	21 %	Total carbohydrate 71 g	64 %
Saturated fat 1 g	2 %	Dietary fiber 5 g	
Cholesterol 17 mg		Sugars 5 g	
Sodium 475 mg		Protein 16 g	15 %

% Daily:

Vitamin A, 12 %; Vitamin C, 62 %; Calcium, 15 %; Iron, 23 %   135

DESI ARNAZ JR.
Desi and Amy's Pasta Delight

2 Servings

1 serving cooking spray (1 second spray)

2 tablespoons Heart Beat* canola oil

¼ cup fresh chives, snipped

3 garlic cloves, peeled and minced

1 cup chopped broccoli

1 cup chopped asparagus

2 cups chopped Chinese cabbage

1 pound whole-wheat pasta, boiled and drained

¾ cup tomato chunks

1 ounce* fresh cilantro (about a handful)

1 ounce* fresh dillweed (about a handful)

Fresh lime juice to taste

Coat wok with cooking spray. Simmer the chives and garlic in oil, about 2 minutes. Turn heat to medium-high and add broccoli, asparagus, and Chinese cabbage, stirring frequently. Add a little water if mixture seems too dry. When broccoli turns dark green—after about 3 minutes—add fresh cooked pasta. Throw in a handful each of chopped tomatoes, cilantro, and dill or other herbs of your choice. Stir and remove from heat. Allow it to rest 2 minutes before serving. Garnish with freshly squeezed lime juice. Enjoy!

The American Heart Association and the surgeon general recommend a maximum daily fat intake of no more than 30 percent, but optimally the intake should be closer to 10 or 20 percent. One way to significantly reduce fat intake is to make the side dishes the main course—load up on vegetables, grains, and legumes. Another way is to use animal foods very sparingly, if at all, as a flavoring or condiment.

Nutritional Analysis   *for 1 serving {854 g}*

Calories 545   Calories from fat 161

Nutrient:	% Calories from:	Nutrient:	% Calories from:
Total fat 18 g	28 %	Total carbohydrate 79 g	55 %
Saturated fat 2 g	2 %	Dietary fiber 14 g	
Cholesterol 0 mg		Sugars 11 g	
Sodium 254 mg		Protein 26 g	18 %

% Daily:

Vitamin A, 71 %; Vitamin C, 486 %; Calcium, 42 %; Iron, 42 %

CAROL BURNETT
Vegetable Medley

4 Servings

1 large zucchini or 2 small ones, enough to make 1½ cups, chopped

1 pound canned corn or the kernels from 2 ears of fresh corn

⅓ pound fresh mushrooms

2 or 3 ripe tomatoes, peeled and cored

6–8 scallions

2 teaspoons Crisco* butter-flavored shortening

½ teaspoon salt

½ teaspoon pepper

Chop zucchini; drain corn; slice mushrooms. Cut tomatoes into large cubes. Slice onions in 1-inch pieces. Melt butter-flavored shortening in skillet. Add zucchini, corn, mushrooms, and salt and pepper to taste. Cook 1 minute, stirring to coat and mix well. Add scallions, cover, and cook about 1 minute more. Add tomatoes, cover, and cook about 5 minutes, stirring occasionally. Serve while hot. *Suggestion:* Serve over Willard Scott's Baked Rice. Garnish with fresh herbs.

It takes five pounds of vegetable protein to produce one pound of chicken protein, seven and a half pounds to produce a pound of pork, and sixteen pounds for every pound of feedlot beef. One and one-third billion people could be fed on the amount of grains and soybeans used to feed the livestock in the U.S. alone. . . . Still, sixty million people starve to death every year.

Nutritional Analysis   for 1 serving {323 g}

Calories 195   Calories from fat 36

Nutrient:	% Calories from:	Nutrient:	% Calories from:
Total fat 4 g	16 %	Total carbohydrate 40 g	72 %
Saturated fat 1 g	3 %	Dietary fiber 6 g	
Cholesterol 0 mg		Sugars 7 g	
Sodium 300 mg		Protein 6 g	11 %

% Daily:

Vitamin A, 10 %; Vitamin C, 56 %; Calcium, 4 %; Iron 12 %

DYAN CANNON
Broccoli-Farfel Stuffing

4 Servings

2 teaspoons Crisco* butter-flavored shortening

1 cup chopped onions

½ pound mushrooms, coarsely chopped

2 garlic cloves, crushed

10 ounces frozen broccoli, thawed

1½ cups matzoh meal farfel

3 servings egg substitute, prepared

1 tablespoon Nucoa Smart Beat* low-fat margarine

½ teaspoon salt

2 teaspoons fresh basil leaves, chopped

⅛ teaspoon black pepper

Melt shortening in skillet.

Sauté onions until soft. Add mushrooms and garlic; sauté until most of the liquid has evaporated. Transfer to medium bowl and allow to cool. Stir in chopped broccoli and farfel. Mix prepared egg substitute and melted reduced-fat margarine and add to broccoli-farfel mixture. Stir in seasonings. *Note:* You may use 1 teaspoon ground basil if fresh is not available. Put the broccoli-farfel mixture into a casserole dish and bake at 350°F for 30–40 minutes or until done.

Nutritional Analysis   *for 1 serving {227 g}*

Calories 154   Calories from fat 30

Nutrient:	% Calories from:	Nutrient:	% Calories from:
Total fat 3 g	15 %	Total carbohydrate 35 g	72 %
Saturated fat 1 g	3 %	Dietary fiber 4 g	
Cholesterol 0 mg		Sugars 3 g	
Sodium 317 mg		Protein 6 g	13 %

% Daily:

Vitamin A, 15 %; Vitamin C, 118 %; Calcium, 5 %; Iron, 8 %

CAPTAIN KANGAROO
Vegetable Casserole

6 Servings

Cooking spray
1 teaspoon salt
¼ teaspoon black pepper
1 teaspoon paprika
1½ cups minced onion
4 large, firm tomatoes
2 cups diced potatoes
1 cup chopped celery
1 cup sliced carrots
2 tablespoons Nucoa Heart Beat* or low-fat margarine

Preheat oven to 375°F. Lightly coat a casserole dish with cooking spray. Combine salt, pepper, and paprika in a small bowl. Slice tomatoes into 1/2-inch slices. Layer the veggies and onions into the casserole dish, sprinkling each layer with seasoning mixture. Dot with margarine; cover and bake for 1 hour or until tender. Incredible!

Five of the leading causes of disease in the United States are diet related. The Standard American Diet (SAD) contributes to heart disease, cancer, obesity, high blood pressure, diabetes, osteoporosis, arthritis, kidney stones, fatigue, high cholesterol, and strokes—and reduces the body's natural antibiotic immunity.

Nutritional Analysis *for 1 serving {281 g}*
Calories 123   Calories from fat 14

Nutrient:	% Calories from:	Nutrient:	% Calories from:
Total fat 2 g	11 %	Total carbohydrate 26 g	78 %
Saturated fat 0 g	1 %	Dietary fiber 5 g	
Cholesterol 0 mg		Sugars 6 g	
Sodium 448 mg		Protein 4 g	11 %

% Daily:
Vitamin A, 112 %; Vitamin C, 64 %; Calcium, 5 %; Iron, 11 %

LYNDA CARTER
Caesar Salad

4 Servings

½ teaspoon* salt

4 garlic cloves, peeled and pressed

¼ teaspoon* black pepper

1 tablespoon miso paste

1 tablespoon capers, minced

1/4 cup* lemon juice (juice of 1 lemon)

2½ tablespoons Angostura* Worcestershire sauce

1 tablespoon Grey Poupon Dijon mustard

2 tablespoons olive oil

¼ cup red wine vinegar

2 tablespoons water

6 cups romaine lettuce leaves

2 Ener-G* egg substitutes

½ cup fat-free croutons

3 tablespoons fat-free Parmesan cheese

Salt the bottom of a wooden salad bowl. Add garlic, black pepper, miso, and capers, working all into a paste. Add lemon juice, Worcestershire, and Dijon mustard. Work into bowl, adding additional pepper to taste. Shake oil, vinegar, and water together vigorously. Sprinkle on sides of bowl. Break up lettuce and place in bowl. Whisk egg substitute until slightly frothy and drizzle over lettuce. Add croutons and Parmesan, tossing thoroughly. Serve immediately.

> For every 1 percent your blood cholesterol rises, your risk of heart attack goes up 2 percent. Over time, eating an egg a day will cause your blood cholesterol to rise 12 percent and your risk of heart attack by 24 percent. Use egg substitutes to reduce the amount of cholesterol in food you prepare.

Nutritional Analysis   for 1 serving {174 g}

Calories 139   Calories from fat 67

Nutrient:	% Calories from:	Nutrient:	% Calories from:
Total fat 7 g	48 %	Total carbohydrate 13 g	38 %
Saturated fat 1 g	6 %	Dietary fiber 2 g	
Cholesterol 4 mg		Sugars 2 g	
Sodium 786 mg		Protein 5 g	13 %

% Daily:

Vitamin A, 22 %; Vitamin C, 54 %; Calcium, 5 %; Iron, 10 %

PHOEBE CATES
Saffron Risotto With Wild Mushrooms and Arugula

DIET IS A FOUR-LETTER WORD! Diets fail because the focus is on weight instead of health. Give up counting calories forever by eating wholesome, vegetarian foods, which are naturally low in fat and have no cholesterol.

4 Servings

2 cups vegetable bouillon

5 grams saffron (pinch)

1 tablespoon butter-flavored Crisco* shortening

6 ounces minced onion (1 small)

1 garlic clove, crushed

1½ cups Arborio rice

½ cup dry white wine

2 servings Pam* cooking spray, olive-oil flavor

1 tablespoon olive oil

4 ounces fresh arugula (1 packed cup)

6 ounces fresh wild mushrooms (1 cup)

½ teaspoon* salt

½ teaspoon* white pepper

½ cups grated Parmesan or pecorino cheese

Heat the stock in a small saucepan, add the saffron, and allow to infuse for 10 minutes. Melt the shortening in a medium skillet. Sauté the onion and garlic for 5 minutes over low heat or until soft. Add the rice and stir over medium heat for 2–3 minutes, or until rice is opaque. Pour in wine; simmer rapidly until most of the liquid has evaporated. Add a third of the warm stock, stir once, and simmer very gently over low heat until liquid is absorbed. Repeat this process twice with the remaining stock until the rice is tender, about 25 minutes. Just before the rice is cooked, in a small skillet coated with cooking spray, heat the oil and stir-fry the mushrooms about 4–5 minutes. Add arugula stirring briefly until just wilted. Stir into the rice, along with the Parmesan cheese, salt, and plenty of pepper. Serve immediately.

Nutritional Analysis   *for 1 serving {357 g}*

Calories 402   Calories from fat 82

Nutrient:	% Calories from:	Nutrient:	% Calories from:
Total fat 9 g	20 %	Total carbohydrate 68 g	65 %
Saturated fat 1 g	3 %	Dietary fiber 1 g	
Cholesterol 10 mg		Sugars 1 g	
Sodium 879 mg		Protein 12 g	11 %

% Daily:

Vitamin A, 7 %; Vitamin C, 5 %; Calcium, 6 %; Iron, 3 %

MARGE CHAMPION
Stuffed Nutted Squash

2 Servings

1 acorn squash

⅜ cup pecans

1 small onion, chopped

1 tablespoon fresh parsley, chopped

½ cup Craneberry's* dried cranberries

1 cup orange juice

Preheat oven to 375°F. Cut squash in half and scrape out seeds. Brown pecans under broiler of toaster oven or regular oven for 2 minutes. Chop pecans and mix with onion, parsley, and dried cranberries. Set squash halves on a baking sheet and stuff with nut mixture. Pour orange juice into each half. Bake 45 minutes to an hour, or until fork easily pierces flesh. Serve hot and enjoy.

Tips: You may need to trim a ridge on the bottom of the squash so it will stand upright (but not too much or it will leak!) Browning the pecans enhances the flavor so you can use less, but watch closely while browning them, because they burn easily. Line baking sheet with aluminum foil or parchment paper to prevent squash from sticking.

Nutritional Analysis   *for 1 serving {348 g}*

Calories 369   Calories from fat 128

Nutrient:	% Calories from:	Nutrient:	% Calories from:
Total fat 14 g	33 %	Total carbohydrate 61 g	62 %
Saturated fat 1 g	3 %	Dietary fiber 8 g	
Cholesterol 0 mg		Sugars 40 g	
Sodium 9 mg		Protein 4 g	5 %

% Daily:

Vitamin A, 9 %; Vitamin C, 135 %; Calcium, 9 %; Iron, 11 %

CHEVY CHASE
Chevy and Jayni's Vegetable Lasagne

8 Servings

1 pound Health Valley* curly-edge lasagne (1 box)

2 pounds broccoli, chopped

2 teaspoons olive oil

4 medium zucchini, chopped

1 medium onion, chopped

2 garlic cloves, peeled and minced

28 ounces Health Valley* low-sodium tomatoes

½ teaspoon salt*

3 cups Frigo* nonfat ricotta cheese

½ cup Weight Watchers* non-fat Parmesan cheese

1 teaspoon oregano

12 ounces Health Valley* nonfat mozzarella, shredded

1 8-ounce jar Health Valley* spaghetti sauce

Preheat oven 350°F. Cook lasagne noodles according to package directions. Steam broccoli 2 minutes. Heat the olive oil and sauté zucchini together with onion, garlic, broccoli, tomatoes, and salt over high heat, stirring constantly, about 5 minutes. In a large bowl combine ricotta, Parmesan, oregano, and shredded mozzarella thoroughly. Heat spaghetti sauce. In a baking dish (about 13 by 9 inches), spread half of the sauce. Layer noodles, tomato-veggie mixture, and cheese mixture. Repeat layers, ending with a layer of lasagne and the other half of the spaghetti sauce on top. Bake 45 minutes. *Suggestion:* Serve with extra Parmesan if desired, and with crusty bread and a crunchy green salad.

Nutritional Analysis   *for 1 serving {544 g}*

Calories 407   Calories from fat 27

Nutrient:	% Calories from:	Nutrient:	% Calories from:
Total fat 3 g	6 %	Total carbohydrate 68 g	58 %
Saturated fat 1 g	2 %	Dietary fiber 13 g	
Cholesterol 18 mg		Sugars 8 g	
Sodium 573 mg		Protein 42 g	36 %

% Daily:

Vitamin A, 50 %; Vitamin C, 226 %; Calcium, 31 %; Iron, 39 %   143

JULIE CHRISTIE
Vegetable Cottage Pie

8 Servings

2 pounds potatoes, diced

½ cup skim milk

2 large onions, peeled and chopped

2 garlic cloves, peeled and minced

1 teaspoon corn oil

2 tablespoons brewer's yeast

14 ounces canned whole tomatoes

1¼ cups white wine

2 tablespoons mixed herbs (handful)

½ teaspoon salt

⅓ cup minced celery

¼ teaspoon chili powder or 1 small chili pepper

1 cup dry-roasted mixed nut pieces, toasted

¼ pound fat-free Cheddar

Steam, boil, or microwave potatoes; when tender, mash with milk. Preheat oven to 375°F. Sauté onion and garlic in oil; add yeast and tomatoes and simmer until yeast is dissolved. Add wine, herbs, salt, celery, and chili (use a small, dried whole chili if you like it hot). Stir into bowl with nuts, which you may first brown under a broiler to enhance flavor, and mix thoroughly. Put in a baking dish and cover with mashed potatoes. Sprinkle top with cheese. Bake as long as it takes to brown top nicely, about 30 minutes.

It is a sad and telling commentary that at a time when more than a billion people are chronically suffering from hunger, 75 percent of the corn, barley, oats, and sorghum imported to Third World countries are fed not to their people but to livestock raised for export.

Nutritional Analysis   *for 1 serving {342 g}*

Calories 288   Calories from fat 89

Nutrient:	% Calories from:	Nutrient:	% Calories from:
Total fat 10 g	31 %	Total carbohydrate 33 g	45 %
Saturated fat 1 g	4 %	Dietary fiber 8 g	
Cholesterol 0 mg		Sugars 4 g	
Sodium 301 mg		Protein 11 g	16 %

% Daily:

Vitamin A, 11 %; Vitamin C, 50 %; Calcium, 22 %; Iron, 42 %

Aunt Carol's Banana Wanana Nutty Wuddy Bread

You can reduce the amount of fat in cakes and brownies baked goods by substituting frozen apple juice concentrate for butter or shortening measure for measure. Prune butter or strained baby food prunes also works well in brownies and chocolate cakes. You'll never miss the fat!

12 Servings

1 serving cooking spray (1 second spray)

1 teaspoon flour

1¾ cups flour

2 teaspoons baking powder

½ teaspoon cinnamon

½ teaspoon nutmeg

½ teaspoon salt

2 ripe bananas, mashed (1 cup)

¾ cups sugar

2 egg substitutes (*Ener-G*)

¼ cup frozen apple juice concentrate

¼ cup skim milk

¾ cup almond pieces, toasted

4 ounces butterscotch chips, chopped

½ cup fat-free margarine (*Promise Ultra*)

3 ounces fat-free cream cheese

1 teaspoon vanilla

1 cup powdered sugar

Preheat oven to 350°F. Coat 2 loaf pans with cooking spray and dust lightly with flour. Sift flour, baking powder and soda, cinnamon, nutmeg and salt together. Combine bananas, sugar, prepared egg substitutes, and frozen apple juice concentrate. Alternately blend in flour mixture and milk. Stir in nuts and butterscotch pieces, reserving a few for topping. Turn mixture into prepared loaf pans. Sprinkle remaining nuts and butterscotch pieces on top. Bake for about 40 minutes. For frosting, blend margarine with cream cheese until smooth. Beat in vanilla and powdered sugar. When cake has cooled, drizzle frosting on top. Incredibly delicious!

Nutritional Analysis   *for 1 serving {122 g}*

Calories 290   Calories from fat 57

Nutrient: % Calories from:		Nutrient: % Calories from:	
Total fat 6 g	19 %	Total carbohydrate 53 g	72 %
Saturated fat 0 g	1 %	Dietary fiber 2 g	
Cholesterol 2 mg		Sugars 26 g	
Sodium 311 mg		Protein 6 g	8 %

% Daily:

Vitamin A, 11 %; Vitamin C, 19 %; Calcium, 7 %; Iron, 8 %

TIM CONWAY
Chicory and Kidney Bean Salad

4 Servings

2 heads of chicory

1 16-ounce can red kidney beans

1 medium onion, minced

1 tablespoon olive oil

3 tablespoons red wine vinegar (or 2 tablespoons vinegar and 1 tablespoon water)

½ teaspoon salt

¼ teaspoon white pepper

Wash the chicory and discard the tough outer leaves. Spin or pat leaves dry. Pour kidney beans and liquid into a bowl and mash into a paste. Add onion, oil, vinegar, and salt and pepper to taste. Arrange chicory in a salad bowl, add the bean mixture, and toss until mixed. *Suggestions:* Try this with tortillas and Joanna Kerns's Salsa. Terrific!

Most doctors and nutrition experts agree that a modified form of vegetarianism is the healthiest way to eat. Now it's easier to change your eating habits than ever before, but don't make too many changes at once. For starters, look for healthier versions of old favorites such as pizza, hamburgers, and hot dogs in the supermarkets. Simplify your mornings— eat fruit or nonfat yogurt for breakfast. Snack on low-fat granola or pretzels instead of junk food.

Nutritional Analysis   *for 1 serving {390 g}*

Calories 220   Calories from fat 35

Nutrient: % Calories from:		Nutrient: % Calories from:	
Total fat 4 g	15 %	Total carbohydrate 35 g	62 %
Saturated fat 0 g	2 %	Dietary fiber 6 g	
Cholesterol 0 mg		Sugars 1 g	
Sodium 313 mg		Protein 13 g	23 %

% Daily:

Vitamin A, 0 %; Vitamin C, 5 %; Calcium, 8 %; Iron, 19 %

DORIS DAY
Sicilian Cheese Casserole

6 Servings

2 cups tiny shell pasta

1 medium eggplant, pared and cut in ½-inch cubes

1 small onion, chopped

1 tablespoon olive oil

3 ounces tomato sauce

¼ teaspoon salt

2 garlic cloves, crushed

1½ cups nonfat Parmesan

2 tablespoons lemon juice

2 ounces fresh parsley

4 tablespoons capers, minced

½ teaspoon basil

½ teaspoon marjoram

6 ounces low-fat Monterey Jack cheese

1 teaspoon black pepper

Preheat oven to 375°F. Cook tiny shell pasta until not quite done (it will finish during baking) and drain. Sprinkle salt on eggplant cubes and allow to "sweat" 10–15 minutes. (Sweating the eggplant lessens the amount of oil required to sauté it.) Sauté eggplant and onions in oil over medium heat until tender. Combine with pasta, tomato sauce, parsley, lemon juice, capers, Parmesan cheese, and seasonings. Transfer to a 2-quart baking dish. Top with sliced Monterey Jack cheese and bake uncovered for 30 minutes.

Nutritional Analysis   *for 1 serving {217 g}*

Calories 322   Calories from fat 74

Nutrient:	% Calories from:	Nutrient:	% Calories from:
Total fat 8 g	22 %	Total carbohydrate 43 g	51 %
Saturated fat 3 g	9 %	Dietary fiber 1 g	
Cholesterol 40 mg		Sugars 4 g	
Sodium 755 mg		Protein 24 g	28 %

% Daily:

Vitamin A, 7 %; Vitamin C, 28 %; Calcium, 4 %; Iron, 13 %

LYNDA DAY-GEORGE
Potatoes Lynda

4 Servings

4 medium, evenly shaped potatoes

1 teaspoon salt

3 tablespoons Nucoa Smart Beat* low-fat margarine, melted

3 tablespoons parsley or herbs of your choice

4 tablespoons grated Kraft Cracker Barrel* low-fat sharp Cheddar cheese

4 tablespoons nonfat grated Parmesan cheese

2 teaspoons paprika

Preheat oven to 425°F. Scrub the potatoes. Cut across potato in 1/8–1/4-inch slices, leaving about 1/4 inch at base, so the potato stays together. Put potatoes on a baking dish and spread open a little. Combine salt, margarine, and 2 tablespoons of the herbs and drizzle into grooves. Top with remaining herbs. Bake for 45–50 minutes. Remove from oven, sprinkle on cheeses and paprika. Return to oven for about 12 minutes or until golden brown. *Variation:* Use 1 1/2 teaspoons caraway seeds or cumin in place of herbs. *Suggestions:* Serve with Geraldo's Green Banana Salad. *Tip:* Lay a wooden spoon handle alongside the potato to prevent the knife from cutting all the way through.

Eating healthy is a continuing process, not an all-or-none affair. Take it a little at a time. Turn three of your old favorite, but fatty, recipes into healthy, low-fat new favorites. Plan a vegetarian day once a week. Get the whole family involved in choosing what to eat that day. And drink water—one of the most important things you can do for your skin.

*Pray for peace and grace
   and spiritual food,
For wisdom and guidance,
   for all these are good,
But don't forget the
   potatoes.*
—John Tyler Petee

Nutritional Analysis   *for 1 serving {262 g}*

Calories 201   Calories from fat 29

Nutrient:	% Calories from:	Nutrient:	% Calories from:
Total fat 3 g	13 %	Total carbohydrate 35 g	66 %
Saturated fat 1 g	4 %	Dietary fiber 7 g	
Cholesterol 10 mg		Sugars 1 g	
Sodium 448 mg		Protein 11 g	21 %

% Daily:
Vitamin A, 21 %; Vitamin C, 52 %; Calcium, 24 %; Iron, 64 %

DOM DELUISE
Stuffed and Rolled Eggplant Marinara

8 Servings

2 servings olive oil cooking spray (2 seconds of spray)

1 tablespoon olive oil

5 garlic cloves, peeled and minced

6 ounces tomato paste

5 pounds tomatoes, blanched and peeled

10 basil leaves, shredded into small pieces

½ teaspoon black pepper

4 ounces Weight Watchers* fat-free Parmesan cheese

2 large eggplants, peeled

1 ounce parsley, chopped fine

1 pound Frigo* fat-free ricotta cheese

½ cup all-purpose wheat flour

2 egg substitutes, prepared

2 servings olive oil cooking spray

½ pound Healthy Choice* nonfat mozzarella cheese, sliced thin

4 ounces Weight Watchers* fat-free Parmesan cheese

For marinara sauce: Heat olive oil in a frying pan coated with cooking spray and sauté garlic. Stir in tomato paste and tomatoes. Cook over medium heat for 20–30 minutes, stirring occasionally. Sprinkle with shredded basil. Add pepper and grated cheese to taste. Remove from heat. For stuffed eggplant: Preheat oven to 350°F. Stir parsley into ricotta and set aside. Slice peeled eggplants lengthwise in 1/4-inch slices. Sprinkle with salt and allow to "sweat" for 10 minutes. Dip in egg substitute, dredge in cracker meal, and bake for 10–15 minutes, or until tender. Place a mozzarella slice and a scoop of ricotta in the middle of each eggplant slice. Roll up and place, seam side down, in a baking pan coated lightly with cooking spray. Cover with marinara sauce. Bake 25–30 minutes. Allow to set up before serving. Garnish with parsley and grated cheese. *Suggestions:* Serve with salad and bread or pasta.

Nutritional Analysis   *for 1 serving {551 g}*

Calories 309   Calories from fat 31

Nutrient:	% Calories from:	Nutrient:	% Calories from:
Total fat 3 g	9 %	Total carbohydrate 46 g	54 %
Saturated fat 0 g	1 %	Dietary fiber 5 g	
Cholesterol 32 mg		Sugars 12 g	
Sodium 514 mg		Protein 31 g	36 %

% Daily:
Vitamin A, 49 %; Vitamin C, 117 %; Calcium, 16 %; Iron, 15 %   149

PHYLLIS DILLER
Parmesan Eggplant Casserole

6 Servings

2 servings cooking spray (2 seconds of spray)

2 large eggplants

⅛ teaspoon salt

½ cup Nucoa Smart Beat* low-fat margarine

1 cup onion, minced

1 bell pepper, minced

2 teaspoons parsley, minced

1¾ cups fat-free Parmesan cheese

16 ounces canned stewed tomatoes

½ teaspoon salt

½ teaspoon black pepper

⅓ cup cracker meal

⅓ teaspoon paprika

Preheat oven to 350°F. Coat a casserole dish lightly with cooking spray. Peel eggplants and chop coarsely; sprinkle with salt and allow to "sweat" for 10–15 minutes. Melt margarine in skillet, add eggplant, onions, bell pepper, simmer 15 minutes. Add parsley, 4 ounces of the cheese, and tomatoes. Simmer 5 more minutes, add salt and pepper, and place in casserole. Combine cracker meal, paprika and remaining cheese, and sprinkle on top of casserole. Bake for 20 minutes. *Suggestion*: Great with crusty bread and leafy salad. *Tip:* Freezes well before baking.

Teens and young adults are among the fastest-growing groups of new vegetarians. They're turning the tables on their parents, telling them to eat their vegetables. Compassion for animals, environmental reasons, weight loss, and better health are the most frequently cited reasons for going meat-free.

Nutritional Analysis   *for 1 serving {290 g}*

Calories 172   Calories from fat 12

Nutrient:	% Calories from:	Nutrient:	% Calories from:
Total fat 1 g	6 %	Total carbohydrate 30 g	65 %
Saturated fat 0 g	1 %	Dietary fiber 1 g	
Cholesterol 23 mg		Sugars 8 g	
Sodium 377 mg		Protein 13 g	28 %

% Daily:

Vitamin A, 17 %; Vitamin C, 83 %; Calcium, 4 %; Iron, 10 %

JULIA DUFFY
Herbed Zucchini Latkes with Roasted Peppers

6 Servings

1 pound zucchini, grated medium fine

½ teaspoon salt

3 tablespoons grated onion

1 large red bell pepper

2 egg substitutes, frothy

½ cup fat-free Parmesan cheese

4 oz skim milk

1 teaspoon rosemary

1 teaspoon chopped basil

2 teaspoons minced fresh herbs

½ teaspoon salt

¼ teaspoon Tabasco sauce

½ teaspoon black pepper

½ cup all-purpose flour

1 teaspoon baking powder

2 tablespoons olive oil

½ cup nonfat yogurt

Sprinkle zucchini with salt and set aside for 1 hour. Drain and squeeze out excess liquid. Cut bell pepper into quarters, removing seeds. Roast under broiler until skin is blistery and beginning to turn brown all over. When cool enough to handle, remove skin and mince flesh. Mix zucchini, onion, and 2 tablespoons of the red pepper, and set aside. In a medium mixing bowl, combine egg, cheese, milk, herbs, salt, Tabasco, and pepper to taste. Sift flour and baking powder together. Add veggies to egg mixture, sift flour again, into the veggies, mixing thoroughly. Heat a little oil in a skillet

---

Nutritional Analysis   *for 1 serving {182 g}*

Calories 147   Calories from fat 46

Nutrient: % Calories from:		Nutrient: % Calories from:	
Total fat 5 g	30 %	Total carbohydrate 20 g	52 %
Saturated fat 1 g	4 %	Dietary fiber 1 g	
Cholesterol 7 mg		Sugars 5 g	
Sodium 282 mg		Protein 7 g	18 %

% Daily:

Vitamin A, 5 %; Vitamin C, 14 %; Calcium, 10 %; Iron, 8 %

over medium-high heat. Spoon mixture into skillet, pressing to form thin 3-inch round latkes. Lightly brown both sides; drain on absorbent paper. Wipe and add oil as needed. Purée remaining red pepper with yogurt. Serve latkes with a spoonful of pepper sauce on top. *Suggestions:* Peppers can be bought or made ahead of time. Latkes can be made in advance: drain, place on a cookie sheet, and store in the refrigerator covered; reheat at 350°F, uncovered.

MICKEY GILLEY
Marshmallow Sweet Potatoes

6 Servings

4 cups hot mashed sweet potatoes

¼ cup Nucoa Smart Beat* low-fat margarine

¼ cup orange juice

½ teaspoon salt

2 cups (4 ounces Emes* gelatin-free miniature marshmallows

Preheat oven to 350°F. To the mashed sweet potatoes, add margarine, orange juice, and salt. Whip in 1 cup of the marshmallows. Place in a 1 1/2-quart casserole and bake for 20 minutes. Top with remaining marshmallows and return to oven until lightly browned. Allow to cool slightly before serving.

If you think you need the calcium in milk to build strong bones, you may be in for a surprise! Stronger bones are more correlated with low protein intake than with amount of calcium. The more milk consumed, the more calcium is lost in urine, resulting in loss of bone density and weak bones. In fact, consumption of animal protein like milk is the single best predictor of osteoporosis!

Nutritional Analysis *for 1 serving {131 g}*

Calories 187   Calories from fat 13

Nutrient:	% Calories from:	Nutrient:	% Calories from:
Total fat 1 g	7 %	Total carbohydrate 42 g	89 %
Saturated fat 0 g	0 %	Dietary fiber 2 g	
Cholesterol 0 mg		Sugars 10 g	
Sodium 264 mg		Protein 2 g	4 %

% Daily:

Vitamin A, 10 %; Vitamin C, 27 %; Calcium, 2 %; Iron, 5 %

AMY GRANT
Sugar Cookies

60 Servings (5 dozen cookies)

1 cup Nucoa Smart Beat*
low-fat margarine

1 cup sugar

4 Ener-G* egg substitutes

3 cups self-rising flour

2 teaspoons Borden's Eagle
Brand* low-fat sweetened
condensed milk

3 servings cooking spray
(3-second spray)

Preheat oven to 375°F. Spray cookie sheet with cooking spray. Cream shortening until soft. Add sugar gradually, creaming after each addition. Blend in egg substitutes and half the flour. Add milk and work in remaining flour, mixing well. Drop by teaspoonfuls onto sprayed cookie sheet. Bake 10–12 minutes. *Variations:* Sprinkle extra sugar on top or decorate with candied fruit, dates, raisins, or nuts. *Tip:* Turn cookie sheet halfway through baking.

Ordering a vegetarian meal in a restaurant used to mean a platter of overcooked vegetables. Now multicourse vegetarian meals are fairly standard at higher-end restaurants across the country. Fast-food restaurants are jumping on the bandwagon, too. Look for new, healthier alternatives at TGI Fridays, Burger King, and Wendy's.

Nutritional Analysis *for 1 cookie (16 g)*

Calories 42   Calories from fat 6

Nutrient:	% Calories from:	Nutrient:	% Calories from:
Total fat 1 g	14 %	Total carbohydrate 8 g	80 %
Saturated fat 0 g	0 %	Dietary fiber 1 g	
Cholesterol 0 mg		Sugars 3 g	
Sodium 108 mg		Protein 1 g	6 %

% Daily:
Vitamin A, 4 %; Vitamin C, 0 %; Calcium, 2 %; Iron 1 %

TIPPI HEDREN

☆ Hot Artichoke Dip

20 Servings

1 14-ounce can artichoke hearts

1 cup Kraft fat-free mayonnaise

1 garlic clove, minced

1¼ cups fat-free Parmesan cheese

Preheat oven to 350°F. Drain artichokes and chop. Mix all ingredients thoroughly. Spread evenly in a 9-inch round pie tin and bake 20–25 minutes. *Suggestion:* Serve buffet style, with chips or crackers—whatever you like. So delicious you won't believe it's almost fat free!

Compassion for life is an oft-cited reason for adopting a vegetarian lifestyle. At the Shambala Preserve, where compassion for life abounds, Tippi Hendren is "den mother" to more than seventy big cats and elephants cast off from private owners, zoos, and circuses. Direct safari queries or contributions to: Roar Foundation, P.O. Box 189, Acton, CA 93510.

Nutritional Analysis *for 1 serving {38 g}*

Calories 33   Calories from fat 1

Nutrient:	% Calories from:	Nutrient:	% Calories from:
Total fat 0 g (less than 1)	2 %	Total carbohydrate 6 g	71 %
Saturated fat 0 g	0 %	Dietary fiber 1 g	
Cholesterol 5 mg		Sugars 1 g	
Sodium 212 mg		Protein 3 g	27 %

% Daily:

Vitamin A, 0 %; Vitamin C, 3 %; Calcium, 1 %; Iron, 1 %

TIPPI HEDREN
Spinach Dip

20 Servings

1 package frozen chopped spinach

8 ounces fat-free sour cream

1 cup fat-free mayonnaise

½ teaspoon lemon juice

1 teaspoon fat-free Italian salad dressing

6 garlic cloves, crushed

1 tablespoon minced parsley

6 minced shallots

Thaw chopped spinach. Press out excess water. Mix all ingredients together in a medium mixing bowl. Transfer to serving dish. *Suggestions:* Great with crackers, chips, and crudités.

Does an apple a day keep the doctor away? So it would seem. Plant foods contain pharmacologically protective agents powerful in counteracting life-threatening diseases. Just eating a couple of pieces of fresh fruit daily can offset many of the undesirable effects caused by a meat- and dairy-rich diet. Apples, for example, promote digestion, are excellent blood purifiers, and aid in the absorption of iron and calcium.

Nutritional Analysis   *for 1 serving {44 g}*

Calories 25   Calories from fat 0

Nutrient:	% Calories from:	Nutrient:	% Calories from:
Total fat 0 g	1 %	Total carbohydrate 5 g	79 %
Saturated fat 0 g	0 %	Dietary fiber 0 g	
Cholesterol 0 mg		Sugars 0 g	
Sodium 176 mg		Protein 1 g	20 %

% Daily:

Vitamin A, 16 %; Vitamin C, 5 %; Calcium, 4 %; Iron, 2 %

CELESTE HOLM
Tomato-Orange Cream Soup

6 Servings

1 10¾-ounce can condensed tomato soup

9 ounces low-sodium tomato juice

3½ ounces orange juice concentrate

2 tablespoons lemon juice

½ cup evaporated skim milk

3 ounces fat-free whipped topping

This versatile soup may be served hot or cold, as an appetizer or dessert. Whip first four ingredients together, then fold in evaporated skim milk. Serve very cold. To serve hot: heat tomato-orange mixture, then add the milk. Serve with generous dollops of whipped topping.

The theory that plant foods must be paired to get the benefit of complementary proteins is obsolete. The key to getting all the requisite nutrients is eating a variety of grains, legumes, fruits, and vegetables daily, while keeping fats and cholesterol (animal products) to a minimum. For a fairly active person, the proportion of nutrients should approximate 60–70 percent carbohydrates, 20 percent protein and 10–20 percent fat—no easy feat if you're eating meat, which derives 50–90 percent of its calories from fat.

Nutritional Analysis *for 1 serving {147 g}*
Calories 83   from fat 17

Nutrient:	% Calories from:	Nutrient:	% Calories from:
Total fat 2 g	19 %	Total carbohydrate 15 g	69 %
Saturated fat 0 g	2 %	Dietary fiber 1 g	
Cholesterol 1 mg		Sugars 1 g	
Sodium 424 mg		Protein 3 g	12 %

% Daily:
Vitamin A, 6 %; Vitamin C, 77 %; Calcium, 1 %; Iron, 6 %

BOB HOPE
Bob's Favorite Lemon Pie

Check out the revised Food Guide Pyramid put out by the USDA. It's not the same old "four food groups" any more! The bulk of your daily food now should be grains, vegetables, and fruits.

8 Servings

4 tablespoons lemon juice

1 cup sugar

4 Ener-G* egg substitutes, prepared

3 tablespoons cornstarch

1 cup water

2 tablespoons Nucoa Smart Beat* low-fat margarine

1 teaspoon lemon zest (finely grated peel)

⅛ teaspoon salt

1 teaspoon powdered sugar

1 tablespoon water

3 servings Pam* butter-flavored cooking spray

3 ounces phyllo pastry sheets (about 6)

8 tablespoons Redi Wip Lite* low-fat whipped topping

Juice enough lemons to make 4 tablespoons (1 large lemon should be enough). In a double boiler over medium heat, combine sugar, egg replacer, and cornstarch, adding water slowly and stirring constantly until thick, smooth, and translucent (about 10–12 minutes). Stir in margarine, lemon zest, fresh lemon juice, and a pinch of salt. Reduce heat and cook 2–3 minutes, stirring occasionally. Remove from heat and allow to cool to almost room temperature. Preheat oven to 375°F. Dissolve powdered sugar in water. Spray a pie pan generously with butter-flavored cooking spray and press the 6 phyllo pastry sheets into the pie pan, one at a time. Brush sugar water over each phyllo sheet and roll up edges to fit inside pie pan. Brush with the remainder of sugar water. Bake shell 8–10 minutes until nicely browned. When both filling and crust have cooled, spoon filling into crust. Chill. Before serving, top with low-fat whipped topping. *Variation:* Top with strawberries instead of or in addition to whipped topping.

Nutritional Analysis   *for 1 serving {102 g}*

Calories 162   Calories from fat 12

Nutrient:	% Calories from:	Nutrient:	% Calories from:
Total fat 1 g	7 %	Total carbohydrate 37 g	90 %
Saturated fat 0 g	0 %	Dietary fiber 0 g	
Cholesterol 0 mg		Sugars 24 g	
Sodium 138 mg		Protein 1 g	3 %

% Daily:

Vitamin A, 4 %; Vitamin C, 1 %; Calcium, 0 %; Iron, 0 %

KIM HUNTER
Givetch

6 Servings

1 cup carrots, sliced thin

1 cup snap beans, ¾-inch diagonal slices

1 cup potato, diced (optional)

½ cup celery, ½-inch diagonal slices

2 medium tomatoes, peeled and quartered

1 cup zucchini, ½-inch slices

1 cup yellow squash, sliced thin

½ onion, ¼-inch slices

¼ cup each: red and green peppers, in thin strips

3 scallions, ½-inch slices (including green tops)

Half of a cauliflower, cut in florets

½ cup fresh green peas

1 tablespoon chopped parsley

1 cup vegetable broth

1 tablespoon olive oil

3 garlic cloves, minced

2 teaspoons salt

¼ teaspoon bay leaf, crumbled

½ teaspoon each rosemary and chili powder

Preheat oven to 350°F. Combine all vegetables in a casserole dish; mix gently and set aside. Heat the broth over medium-high heat and add oil, minced garlic, salt, bay leaf, remaining herbs (crushed fine), and sesame seeds; bring to a boil. Pour over vegetables and cover tightly (use a layer of foil before putting on cover). Bake for 60–75 minutes, gently mixing twice during cooking. Uncover and sprinkle generously with Parmesan and cover with thinly sliced Monterey Jack cheese. Place under broiler until cheese is bubbly and golden.

Variation: Instead of rosemary, chili, and thyme, use 1/2 teaspoon each of savory and tarragon.

Suggestion: Serve with thickly sliced bread.

Ingredients continued

¼ teaspoon thyme

1 teaspoon sesame seeds

½ cup fat-free Parmesan cheese

¼ pound low-fat Monterey Jack cheese

Nutritional Analysis   *for 1 serving {400 g}*

Calories 205   Calories from fat 57

Nutrient:	% Calories from:	Nutrient:	% Calories from:
Total fat 6 g	26 %	Total carbohydrate 26 g	48 %
Saturated fat 2 g	10 %	Dietary fiber 6 g	
Cholesterol 20 mg		Sugars 9 g	
Sodium 616 mg		Protein 14 g	26 %

% Daily:

Vitamin A, 115 %; Vitamin C, 151 %; Calcium, 38 %; Iron, 14 %   159

WILL HUTCHINS
Corn Pudding

4 Servings

¼ cup onions, chopped

2 tablespoons all-purpose flour

2 tablespoons Nucoa Smart Beat* low-fat margarine

1 cup evaporated skim milk

1 cup corn (canned, frozen, or kernels from 2 ears of fresh corn)

1½ teaspoons salt

¼ teaspoons black pepper

1½ teaspoons sugar

2 Ener-G* egg substitutes

1 cup fresh raspberries

Preheat oven to 350°F.
Sauté onion in 1 tablespoon margarine and set aside.
Melt remaining margarine in saucepan and stir in flour.
Pour milk in slowly, stirring until smooth. Bring to boil, add corn, sautéed onion, sugar, beaten egg substitutes, salt, and pepper. Mix well. Pour into greased 7-inch baking dish. Bake for 35–40 minutes, until lightly browned. Serve chilled for dessert with fresh raspberries.

How much protein is enough? Babies need the most and get all of it from mother's milk, which derives about 6 percent of its calories from protein. Any natural food diet easily provides at least 9 percent. In fact, it's almost impossible to get enough calories and not get enough protein, unless the diet is composed mostly of junkfood.

Nutritional Analysis   *for 1 serving {170 g}*

Calories 148   Calories from fat 19

Nutrient:	% Calories from:	Nutrient:	% Calories from:
Total fat 2 g	13 %	Total carbohydrate 27 g	70 %
Saturated fat 0 g	1 %	Dietary fiber 3 g	
Cholesterol 3 mg		Sugars 6 g	
Sodium 934 mg		Protein 7 g	17 %

% Daily:

Vitamin A, 9 %; Vitamin C, 18 %; Calcium, 2 %; Iron, 3 %

ANNE JEFFREYS
Thomas Jefferson's Chess Pie

8 Servings

3 servings Pam* butter-flavored cooking spray

3 ounces (about 6) Apollo* phyllo pastry sheets

1 teaspoon powdered sugar

1 tablespoon water

1 teaspoon apricot brandy

2 teaspoons apricot preserves

3 ounces chopped pecans

¼ cup Nucoa Smart Beat* low-fat margarine

½ cup sugar

1 cup brown sugar

⅛ teaspoon salt

3 Ener-G* egg substitutes

1 teaspoon vanilla

2 tablespoons all-purpose flour

½ cup evaporated skim milk

Preheat oven to 375°F.

Spray a pie pan generously with butter-flavored cooking spray and press the 6 phyllo pastry sheets into the pie pan, one at a time. Dissolve powdered sugar in water. Brush sugar water over the phyllo and roll up edges to form edge and fit inside pie pan. Brush with remaining sugar water. Blend brandy and apricot preserves until liquefied; paint the pastry with with the apricot glaze. Bake shell about 5–6 minutes until just beginning to brown. Brown pecans slightly in toaster oven or un-der oven broiler to enhance flavor (be careful not to scorch!). Cream margarine to soften. Add sugars and salt, creaming thoroughly. Add prepared egg substitutes a little at a time, beating well after each addition. Stir in vanilla, flour, milk, and pecans. Spoon in filling and bake 40–50 minutes or until knife inserted halfway between edge and middle of filling comes out clean. Don't overbake.

Apricots pack quite a nutritional wallop. Very low in calories, they have virtually no sodium or fat and of course no cholesterol. They are great for digestion and their high potassium content is good for cardiovascular health. Rich in beta carotene, ten dried apricot halves weigh in at only 85 calories but supply 20 percent of the RDA for iron.

Nutritional Analysis   *for 1 serving {102 g}*

Calories 248   Calories from fat 34

Nutrient:	% Calories from:	Nutrient:	% Calories from:
Total fat 4 g	13 %	Total carbohydrate 52 g	82 %
Saturated fat 0 g	1 %	Dietary fiber 0 g	
Cholesterol 1 mg		Sugars 12 g	
Sodium 191 mg		Protein 3 g	4 %

% Daily:

Vitamin A, 8 %; Vitamin C, 0 %; Calcium, 2 %; Iron, 3 %

JAMES EARL JONES
Fettuccine Alfredo

6 Servings

¾ pound uncooked fettuccine

3 tablespoons Nucoa Smart Beat* low-fat margarine

1⅓ cups evaporated skim milk

½ teaspoon salt

⅛ teaspoon white pepper

⅛ teaspoon ground nutmeg

1 cup Weight Watchers* fat-free Parmesan cheese

Cook fettuccine in salted water 6–8 minutes, drain, and return it to dry pot. While fettucine is cooking, place margarine and milk in heavy skillet over medium heat. Cook, stirring, for 2 minutes, until well blended and bubbling. Stir in salt, pepper, and nutmeg; remove from heat. Gradually add Parmesan until well blended. Return to heat if necessary to melt cheese. Pour sauce over fettuccine. Toss until well coated. Serve immediately. *Variation:* Toss in a cup of green peas and top with minced scallions.

A major risk factor for arteriosclerosis (hardening of the arteries) is high cholesterol levels. Since all animal foods and no plant foods contain cholesterol, one sensible choice is to minimize the intake of animal foods. This reduces the amount of saturated fat in the diet and helps keep cholesterol levels low. When dairy products are called for, use fat-free varieties.

Nutritional Analysis   for 1 serving {154 g}

Calories 262   Calories from fat 31

Nutrient:	% Calories from:	Nutrient:	% Calories from:
Total fat 3 g	12 %	Total carbohydrate 43 g	64 %
Saturated fat 0 g	0 %	Dietary fiber 0 g	
Cholesterol 26 mg		Sugars 4 g	
Sodium 348 mg		Protein 16 g	24 %

% Daily:

Vitamin A, 9 %; Vitamin C, 0 %; Calcium, 3 %; Iron, 4 %

SHIRLEY JONES AND MARTY INGELS
Marty's Nutty Cheese Roll

16 Servings

8 ounces fat-free cream cheese

1 ounce blue cheese, crumbled

4 ounces shredded Kraft Cracker Barrel* fat-free Cheddar cheese

¼ teaspoon garlic powder

1 tablespoon brandy

1 tablespoon sherry

½ teaspoon Angostura* Worcestershire sauce (dash)

⅛ teaspoon white pepper (dash)

½ cup minced toasted walnuts

½ cup minced toasted almonds

Blend all ingredients except nuts. Form into a ball and roll in the chopped nuts. Cover with plastic wrap and refrigerate for 2 hours. *Tip:* Crumble blue cheese very fine for better distribution.

Nutritional Analysis   *for 1 serving {36 g}*

Calories 80   Calories from fat 39

Nutrient: % Calories from:		Nutrient: % Calories from:	
Total fat 4 g	47 %	Total carbohydrate 3 g	14 %
Saturated fat 1 g	7 %	Dietary fiber 0 g	
Cholesterol 5 mg		Sugars 0 g	
Sodium 177 mg		Protein 7 g	35 %

% Daily:

Vitamin A, 0 %; Vitamin C, 1 %; Calcium, 3 %; Iron 2 %

JOANNA KERNS
My Brother's Salsa

12 Servings

1 pound fresh tomatoes, diced

½ cup water or puréed tomato

¼ teaspoon salt

Juice from half a lime

1 garlic clove, crushed

½ teaspoon olive oil

3 jalapeño peppers* (or to taste)

4 ounces ripe Florida* avocado

1 2-ounce bunch cilantro

1 4-ounce bunch scallions

In a blender, put tomatoes with liquid, salt, lime juice, and garlic. In a pan, heat oil and blacken skins of 1–5 jalapeños (depending on hotness desired). Put some water in a plastic bag, then empty it out—just to dampen the sides of the bag. Put the blackened peppers in the bag and place in the freezer for 5–10 minutes. Remove bag from the freezer and pull the skins from the jalapeños. Add the skinless peppers to blender and blend. Chop cilantro and shallots; dice avocado. Place these three ingredients in a bowl and toss. Pour blended ingredients into bowl and stir. Enjoy! *Suggestions:* Great with fat-free (baked not fried) chips and drizzled over tacos.

The New Four Food Groups (and recommended daily servings) set forth by the Physicians' Committee for Responsible Medicine (PCRM) are: Grains (5 or more servings), Fruits (3 or more), Vegetables (3 or more), and Legumes (2 or 3), with more emphasis placed on these proportions than on the actual serving size. Use of meat and dairy foods is considered optional, but should be kept to a minimum. The PCRM focus is on providing an optimal food guide—one that assures the essentials and avoids the excesses.

Nutritional Analysis   *for 1 serving {82 g}*

Calories 31   Calories from fat 11

Nutrient:	% Calories from:	Nutrient:	% Calories from:
Total fat 1 g	35 %	Total carbohydrate 4 g	53 %
Saturated fat 0 g	6 %	Dietary fiber 1 g	
Cholesterol 0 mg		Sugars 1 g	
Sodium 157 mg		Protein 1 g	12 %

% Daily:

Vitamin A, 7 %; Vitamin C, 23 %; Calcium, 2 %; Iron, 5 %

Note: A Florida avocado derives 66 percent of its calories from fat, compared to 81 percent for California avocados and up to 95 percent for others.
Tip: When handling jalapeños, wear rubber gloves and avoid touching face and eyes.

DEBORAH KERR
Beetroot Cream Soup

6 Servings

1 beetroot (4 ounces*)
½ celery stalk
2 tablespoons Nucoa Smart Beat* low-fat margarine
1½ ounces all-purpose flour
2 cups vegetable stock
1 teaspoon salt
½ teaspoon white pepper
¼ cup evaporated skim milk

Peel, precook, (boiled or steamed) and grate beetroot. Wash, trim, and grate celery. Melt margarine in a saucepan, stir in flour, and cook without browning for a few minutes. Add vegetable stock, stirring until mixture boils. Add beetroot and celery to stock and simmer, covered, for 30 minutes—not more, or the color will be spoiled. Pass soup through a sieve, pressing through enough beetroot to give a good color and consistency. Season carefully to taste and add milk. Heat thoroughly but without letting it boil, otherwise soup will curdle. Serve hot. *Variation:* Add a grated carrot when you add the celery. *Suggestion:* Garnish with fennel fronds.

Beets are amazing! Rich in super-antioxidant Vitamin A, they are great for your skin and help protect you from cancer. They are soothing to the digestive system, but because they are loaded with minerals, especially iron, they're also energizing and help to fight fatigue. Try a sprinkling of grated raw beets on your next green salad for great taste, a nutritional boost, and a splash of vibrant color—all for about 32 calories a cup!

Nutritional Analysis   *for 1 serving {126 g}*
Calories 52   Calories from fat 7

Nutrient:	% Calories from:	Nutrient:	% Calories from:
Total fat 1 g	15 %	Total carbohydrate 8 g	68 %
Saturated fat 0 g	1 %	Dietary fiber 0 g	
Cholesterol 0 mg		Sugars 0 g	
Sodium 561 mg		Protein 2 g	17 %

% Daily:
Vitamin A, 5 %; Vitamin C, 8 %; Calcium, 5 %; Iron, 4 %

DEBORAH KERR
Vegetable Pie

4 Servings

1½ cups onions

2 carrots

2 celery stalks

½ cup mushrooms ("a few")

2 teaspoons flour

1 teaspoon salt

½ teaspoon black pepper

½ cup green peas

½ cup cooked Ancient Harvest* quinoa

¼ cup water

2 teaspoons Nucoa Smart Beat* low-fat margarine

3 servings Pam* butter-flavored cooking spray

3 ounces (about 6) Apollo* phyllo pastry sheets

Preheat oven to 375°F. Mince onions, carrots, celery, and mushrooms. Dust with flour seasoned with salt and pepper. Put into a pan with the peas, quinoa, and very little water. Stew until slightly tender. Transfer to a pie dish. Dot with little dabs of margarine and cover with phyllo sheets. Spray edges of phyllo with cooking spray and roll up to fit pan and form edge. Lightly spray top of pastry with cooking spray. Bake for 30 minutes or until golden. Allow to cool somewhat before serving. *Variation:* Add diced potatoes and fresh herbs—dill is great!

A simple and elegant way to prepare food without fat is en papillote *(in paper), which works on the same principle as oven-baking bags, sealing in all the juices, but each diner gets his own "pot au feu." Mix chopped veggies and seasonings and place on large squares of parchment paper (find it near wax paper at the supermarket). Splash a little water, stock, vegetable juice, or wine on top and seal tightly to hold in steam and juices. Bake in a 400°F oven for 15–25 minutes, depending on the type and size of the veggies. To serve, place on individual plates and slit open.*

Nutritional Analysis   *for 1 serving {189 g}*

Calories 172   Calories from fat 18

Nutrient: % Calories from:		Nutrient: % Calories from:	
Total fat 2 g	10 %	Total carbohydrate 34 g	76 %
Saturated fat 0 g	1 %	Dietary fiber 4 g	
Cholesterol 0 mg		Sugars 5 g	
Sodium 469 mg		Protein 6 g	14 %

% Daily:

Vitamin A, 105 %; Vitamin C, 27 %; Calcium, 4 %; Iron, 6 %

DEBORAH KERR
Walnut Trifle

4 Servings

12 ounces fat-free custard

6 ounces fat-free stale Sara Lee Pound Cake* crumbs

3 ounces walnuts

2 ripe bananas

¼ cup all-fruit raspberry jam

¼ cup cherries, packed in juice

1 tablespoon Angelica dessert wine

Prepare custard and refrigerate until ready to use. Toast walnuts slightly in toaster oven or under oven broiler or to enhance flavor, reserving a few whole nuts for decoration. Pass remainder through a mill or chop fine. Slice the bananas. Mix the cake crumbs, bananas, and most of the chopped nuts with the jam and enough custard to make a fairly firm paste. Place in a dish, cover with remaining custard, and scatter remaining nut pieces on top. Decorate with whole walnuts, cherries, and a drizzle of Angelica or other liqueur.

Nutritional Analysis   *for 1 serving {319 g}*

Calories 507   Calories from fat 108

Nutrient:	% Calories from:	Nutrient:	% Calories from:
Total fat 12 g	21 %	Total carbohydrate 91 g	72 %
Saturated fat 1 g	2 %	Dietary fiber 4 g	
Cholesterol 2 mg		Sugars 19 g	
Sodium 273 mg		Protein 9 g	7 %

% Daily:

Vitamin A, 8 %; Vitamin C, 20 %; Calcium, 20 %; Iron, 9 %

K. D. LANG
Indonesian Salad With Spicy Peanut Dressing

Dr. John McDougall, the low-fat-diet expert, calls potatoes "the ideal weight-loss food." Potatoes are a great source of vitamin C and potassium, which can help curtail high blood pressure. They are a terrific source of fiber and can help lower cholesterol. Cook diced potatoes in your vegetable steamer for a moist delectable flavor that needs no added butter or fat.

6 Servings

2 small potatoes (12 ounces)

1 pound Mori Nu* firm tofu

3 servings cooking spray (3 seconds of spray)

1 tablespoon vegetable oil

¼ teaspoon salt

½ pound spinach

Half of a small cabbage (16 ounces)

½ pound mung beans

Dressing

4 garlic cloves

¼ cup roasted Virginia peanuts

5 teaspoons soy sauce or tamari

1½ tablespoons each of lemon and lime juice

4 teaspoons brown sugar

¼ teaspoon cayenne

2 tablespoons water

Boil or steam potatoes. Press water out of firm tofu and cut into 1/4-inch cubes. Lightly coat medium skillet with cooking spray. Heat 1 teaspoon oil and the salt over medium heat. Add the tofu in small batches, sautéing until lightly browned (about 5 minutes) and adding oil as needed. Remove with slotted spoon and drain on paper towels. Cut boiled or steamed potatoes into bite-size wedges. Wash spinach, cabbage, and mung beans. Steam and chop spinach; shred and lightly steam cabbage. Arrange tofu, potatoes, spinach, and cabbage on individual plates. To prepare dressing, blend garlic, peanuts, soy or tamari sauce, lime-lemon juice, brown sugar, cayenne pepper, and water until smooth. If dressing is too thick, add another teaspoon of water. Top with bean sprouts and dressing, and serve immediately.

Nutritional Analysis   *for 1 serving {314 g}*

Calories 206   Calories from fat 69

Nutrient:	% Calories from:	Nutrient:	% Calories from:
Total fat 8 g	31 %	Total carbohydrate 27 g	47 %
Saturated fat 2 g	7 %	Dietary fiber 4 g	
Cholesterol 0 mg		Sugars 5 g	
Sodium 386 mg		Protein 12 g	22 %

% Daily:

Vitamin A, 27 %; Vitamin C, 100 %; Calcium, 13 %; Iron, 19 %   169

ROBIN LEACH
Cassis Caviar

12 Servings

1 bunch spinach (8 ounces*)

1 medium eggplant (2 cups*)

½ teaspoon* salt

¼ teaspoon* white pepper

2 large onions (2 cups*)

1 teaspoon olive oil

2 sliced tomatoes

1 serving Pam* olive oil cooking spray (1-second spray)

12 ounces Joan Van Ark's REDUXed Broccoli Pesto (page 181)

6 tablespoons Quinoa Caviar (page 171)

4 ounces (about 8 sheets) Apollo* phyllo pastry sheets

2 servings Pam* butter-flavored cooking spray

Preheat oven to 400°F. Clean and steam spinach. Peel and slice eggplant thinly, and season to taste with salt and pepper. Sauté onions in oil until clear. Lightly coat a shallow casserole or pie dish with oil-flavored cooking spray. Alternate layers of eggplant, onions, spinach, tomatoes, and pesto sauce. Repeat layers to top. Center the phyllo sheets on top of the casserole dish. Spray edges lightly with butter-flavored cooking spray and roll up to fit dish and to form edge of pastry. Lightly spray the top with the butter-flavored cooking spray. Bake 20–25 minutes, or until golden. Cut into individual pieces. Garnish each piece with a dab of Quinoa Caviar. *Suggestion:* For special occasions, bake in individual soufflé molds. Garnish with sprigs of fresh oregano.

Once considered a fringe element, vegetarians are right in the mainstream for the next millennium. The vegetarian lifestyle is more simpatico to our beautiful planet and invigorating to ourselves. Today people from all walks of life—doctors, nutritionists, athletes, construction workers, professionals, students—are saying no to dead, devitalized foods and yes to vegetarianism and vibrant good health.

Nutritional Analysis *for 1 serving {130 g}*

Calories 102   Calories from fat 27

Nutrient:	% Calories from:	Nutrient:	% Calories from:
Total fat 3 g	27 %	Total Carbohydrate 14 g	54 %
Saturated fat 0 g	4 %	Dietary fiber 3 g	
Cholesterol 3 mg		Sugars 2 g	
Sodium 401 mg		Protein 5 g	19 %

% Daily:

Vitamin A, 12 %; Vitamin C, 43 %; Calcium, 3 %; Iron, 9 %

Quinoa Caviar

12 Servings

1 cup Ancient Harvest*
quinoa, whole or ground

4 ounces raw wakame (or
other seaweed), dry

2 tablespoons onion, chopped
fine

¼ cup cooked shiitake,
chopped

2½ teaspoons vegetable oil

1 dash Mongolian hot oil

1 tablespoon miso (soybean
paste)

2 tablespoons La Choy Lite*
soy sauce

½ teaspoon sesame oil

> *"The discovery of a new dish does more for the happiness of mankind than the discovery of a new star."*
> —*Jean Anthelme Brillat-Savarin*

Cook wakame or other seaweed with quinoa. Remove seaweed and chop into thin strips. Put aside. Sauté minced onions and shiitake mushrooms in vegetable oil with a dash of Mongolian hot oil for about 4 minutes. In a small bowl, mix miso and soy sauce completely; add to mushrooms and onions, stirring constantly for about 1–2 minutes or until liquid is thick and fairly clear. Mix with quinoa. Makes 12 tablespoons. Serve as any caviar. Garnish with seaweed strips.

Nutritional Analysis *for 1 serving {15 g}*
Calories 28   Calories from fat 8

Nutrient:	*% Calories from:*	*Nutrient:*	*% Calories from:*
Total fat 1 g	27 %	Total carbohydrate 4 g	61 %
Saturated fat 0 g	7 %	Dietary fiber 0 g	
Cholesterol 0 mg		Sugars 0 g	
Sodium 165 mg		Protein 1 g	13 %

% Daily:
Vitamin A, 0 %; Vitamin C, 0 %; Calcium, 0 %; Iron, 1 %

ART LINKLETTER
Minestrone

12 Servings

2 servings cooking spray (2 seconds of spray)

1½ tablespoons olive oil

6 garlic cloves, peeled and chopped

2 large Spanish onions, diced

6 carrots, scraped and diced

3 large celery stalks, sliced

1½ teaspoons salt

1 medium cabbage (2 pounds), shredded

10 large kale leaves (2 ounces), chopped

½ teaspoon thyme

2 bay leaves, broken

3 quarts water

1 28-ounce can plum tomatoes

1 pound chickpeas, cooked

1 cup penne or small shells

½ teaspoon black pepper

½ teaspoon salt

Lightly coat the bottom of a 10-quart pot with cooking spray. Heat olive oil; add garlic, onions, carrots, celery, and 1/2 teaspoon salt, and cook over low heat until onions are wilted but not brown. Add cabbage, kale, thyme, bay leaves, and remaining 1 teaspoon of salt. Increase heat, stirring constantly for about 1 minute; then add water, tomatoes, and chickpeas, and bring to a full boil. Lower heat and simmer, covered, for 45 minutes. Add the pasta and cook for an additional 15 minutes, or until pasta is tender. Season with salt and pepper to taste. *Suggestion:* Serve with a hearty multigrain bread. Garnish with carrot curls or fat-free grated cheese. *Note:* This soup freezes well and is a great "comfort food."

Nutritional Analysis   *for 1 serving {522 g}*

Calories 196   Calories from fat 52

Nutrient:	% Calories from:	Nutrient:	% Calories from:
Total fat 6 g	25 %	Total carbohydrate 32 g	60 %
Saturated fat 1 g	6 %	Dietary fiber 7 g	
Cholesterol 3 mg		Sugars 10 g	
Sodium 452 mg		Protein 8 g	15 %

% Daily:

Vitamin A, 109 %; Vitamin C, 105 %; Calcium, 10 %; Iron, 13 %

HAYLEY MILLS
Pasta With Fresh Tomatoes

8 Servings

3 tablespoons olive oil

3 garlic cloves, peeled and minced

1 cup basil leaves, washed and cut in strips

1 teaspoon salt

½ teaspoon black pepper

4 tomatoes, cubed

8 ounces brie cheese, rind off, cubed

24 ounces linguine, white and green mixed

8 tablespoons fat-free Parmesan cheese

Pour olive oil into mixing bowl and stir in garlic, basil, salt and pepper. Add tomatoes and brie; coat thoroughly, and allow to marinate at least 2 1/2 hours. At mealtime, drop linguine in rapidly boiling water with 1 teaspoon olive oil. Drain and mix with tomatoe/brie elixir: brie should melt! Sprinkle with Parmesan and serve immediately. *Suggestion:* This dish is great with Judy Collins's Grilled Veggies. *Tip:* The olive oil in the boiling water keeps the pasta from sticking, but use some of the oil from the elixir to avoid adding additional fat calories.

Nutritional Analysis   *for 1 serving {196 g}*

Calories 507   Calories from fat 126

Nutrient: % Calories from:		Nutrient: % Calories from:	
Total fat 14 g	26 %	Total carbohydrate 69 g	57 %
Saturated fat 1 g	2 %	Dietary fiber 1 g	
Cholesterol 34 mg		Sugars 2 g	
Sodium 621 mg		Protein 20 g	17 %

% Daily:

Vitamin A, 8 %; Vitamin C, 20 %; Calcium, 8 %; Iron, 21 %   173

JULIE NEWMAR
Eggplant Sauce With Pasta

8 Servings

3 servings cooking spray
(3 seconds of spray)

6 garlic cloves, crushed

18 ounces (3 small cans)
tomato paste

2 medium eggplants (about
2 pounds)

2 small red bell peppers,
seeded and diced

3 cups tomatoes, peeled and
chopped

4 tablespoons capers, minced

2 tablespoons olive oil

1 tablespoon oregano

½ teaspoon basil

¼ teaspoon red pepper flakes

1 cup red wine

2 tablespoons sugar

2 teaspoons salt

1 cup water

24 ounces fresh pasta, cooked
(such as mafalda or linguine)

Lightly coat a skillet with cooking spray. Sauté garlic in oil until golden. Add tomato paste and cook over medium heat about 20 minutes, or until very dark, stirring very often from the bottom. Meanwhile, wash eggplants and chop into 1/2-inch cubes; sprinkle with salt, and allow to "sweat" until ready to use. When tomato paste is a rich, dark color, add peppers, eggplant, tomatoes, and capers, stirring to coat evenly. Stir in remaining ingredients (except pasta), cover, and simmer on medium-low heat for about an hour, stirring occasionally and scraping the bottom to prevent scorching. Add water or extra wine if sauce gets too thick. Serve over fresh-cooked pasta. *Suggestion:* Garnish with fresh rosemary and serve with crusty bread.

If you're not looking forward to the excess weight due to the slowing of metabolic processes that comes with age, perhaps you should consider becoming a vegetarian. Vegetarians have a higher resting metabolic rate than meat-eaters. And they have more circulating norepinephrine, a substance instrumental in the regulation of involuntary responses to stress. Increased metabolism and decreased stress are just two of the numerous benefits of a vegetarian lifestyle.

Nutritional Analysis   *for 1 serving {478 g}*

Calories 303   Calories from fat 53

Nutrient:	% Calories from:	Nutrient:	% Calories from:
Total fat 7 g	17 %	Total carbohydrate 53 g	66 %
Saturated fat 1 g	2 %	Dietary fiber 5 g	
Cholesterol 28 mg		Sugars 8 g	
Sodium 940 mg		Protein 10 g	12 %

% Daily:

Vitamin A, 23 %; Vitamin C, 71 %; Calcium, 8 %; Iron, 23 %

TATUM O'NEAL
Pasta With Tomato Sauce

4 Servings

½ teaspoon salt

1 pound fresh pasta

½ onion, minced

3 teaspoons virgin olive oil

28 ounces canned plum tomatoes, chopped

¼ teaspoon red pepper

1 cup plum tomatoes, peeled and chopped

4 tablespoons fat-free Parmesan cheese

1 teaspoon freshly grated black pepper

8 whole basil leaves

Put salted water on to boil over high heat and add pasta when boiling. Meanwhile, sauté onion in 2 teaspoons of the oil until clear and golden. Add canned plum tomatoes and red pepper, and simmer for 5 minutes. Add fresh tomatoes, stir, and simmer an additional 15 minutes. When pasta is al dente, drain and transfer to a bowl. Toss with remaining teaspoon of the olive oil. Ladle on tomato sauce, add freshly grated Parmesan and black pepper, and garnish with fresh basil leaves.

Myth: IT TAKES MEAT TO MAKE MUSCLE. You don't need meat—you don't even need protein—to make muscle. What you do need is amino acids: the building blocks that combine variously to form the proteins needed by the body. Eating a variety of wholesome foods such as beans, grains, lentils, and vegetables provides all the essential amino acids needed.

Nutritional Analysis   *for 1 serving {402 g}*

Calories 257   Calories from fat 48

Nutrient:	% Calories from:	Nutrient:	% Calories from:
Total fat 5 g	18 %	Total carbohydrate 44 g	66 %
Saturated fat 1 g	2 %	Dietary fiber 4 g	
Cholesterol 38 mg		Sugars 8 g	
Sodium 349 mg		Protein 11 g	16 %

% Daily:

Vitamin A, 16 %; Vitamin C, 71 %; Calcium, 8 %; Iron, 17 %   175

GREGORY PECK
Ratatouille

4 Servings

3 servings cooking spray
(3 seconds of spray)
4 bell peppers
2 large onions
4 tomatoes
1½ pounds eggplant
1 pound zucchini
4 teaspoons olive oil
1 teaspoon salt
1 teaspoon black pepper
2 tablespoons fines herbes
(mixed herbs)

Trim stems from peppers, remove seeds and membrane, and cut into julienne strips. Peel and coarsly chop onions, tomatoes, eggplant, and zucchini. Coat casserole dish with cooking spray. Heat oil over medium high heat in a casserole. Add onions and cook them gently until they are very soft, stirring often so they do not brown. Add chopped vegetables to onions. Season to taste with salt and pepper, and cook over low heat for 30 minutes, stirring occasionally. When veggies are tender, let cool slightly and sprinkle with fines herbes or other herbs of your choice. Serve warm or at room temperature.

You can burn more calories simply by eating more grains, beans, and vegetables. These foods are loaded with complex carbohydrates that trigger the release of natural hormones that increase metabolic rate. Because it is easier for the body to store fat than carbohydrates, you can actually eat more calories and burn more off without lifting anything but your fork!

Nutritional Analysis   *for 1 serving {576 g}*
Calories 195   Calories from fat 61

Nutrient: % Calories from:		Nutrient: % Calories from:	
Total fat 7 g	27 %	Total carbohydrate 34 g	61 %
Saturated fat 1 g	3 %	Dietary fiber 5 g	
Cholesterol 0 mg		Sugars 10 g	
Sodium 559 mg		Protein 7 g	12 %

% Daily:
Vitamin A, 21 %; Vitamin C, 181 %; Calcium, 14 %; Iron, 27 %

GERALDO RIVERA
Hilda's Caramel Custard

8 Servings

1 cup sugar

4 Ener-G* egg substitutes, prepared

1 cup water

14 ounces Eagle Brand Lite* low-fat condensed milk

12 ounces evaporated skim milk

1/2 teaspoon vanilla

Prepare caramel as follows: Place sugar in fireproof bowl over medium heat. Stir until melted (do not burn) and let it cool. Mix all other ingredients well and pour over caramel. Place bowl in a double boiler and cook until knife comes out clean. Cool, then refrigerate for 2 hours before serving. *Suggestions:* Garnish with fresh mint leaves. Serve with raspberries or other fruit in season.

CHECK YOUR FOOD RATIOS. We are basically a vegetarian species and 80–90 percent of our diet should come from plants, says nutrition biochemist T. Colin Campbell of Cornell University. He challenges doctors to tell the public the truth, that "a diet of roots, stems, flowers, fruits, and leaves is the healthiest diet and the only diet we [doctors] can promote, endorse, and recommend."

Nutritional Analysis   *for 1 serving {183 g}*

Calories 350   Calories from fat 26

Nutrient: % Calories from:		Nutrient: % Calories from:	
Total fat 3 g	8 %	Total carbohydrate 72 g	83 %
Saturated fat 2 g	5 %	Dietary fiber 0 g	
Cholesterol 11 mg		Sugars 65 g	
Sodium 126 mg		Protein 8 g	10 %

% Daily:

Vitamin A, 7 %; Vitamin C, 12 %; Calcium, 12 %; Iron, 3 %

FRED ROGERS
Tofu Burgers

8 Servings

1 cup minced onions

3 tablespoons water

20 ounces firm Mori Nu* tofu

2/3 cup crumbs made from whole-wheat melba toast

4 Ener-G* egg substitutes

2 tablespoons Angostura* Worcestershire sauce

1 tablespoon La Choy Lite* soy sauce

½ teaspoon garlic salt

1 tablespoon Crisco Butter Flavor* shortening

Simmer onions in water until tender. Cool. Drain tofu and crumble into medium mixing bowl. Mix in onions, crumbs, eggs, sauces, and seasoning, combining thoroughly. Form into 8 patties and fry in shortening until crisp and evenly browned on both sides. *Variations:* Add a shredded carrot and/or a tablespoon of snipped chives before forming patties. *Suggestion:* Serve on whole-wheat kaiser roll with sprouts.

Every hour 500,000 animals are killed for meat in the United States. The slaughtering methods are gruesome and, although it would cost about a penny extra per animal to make the process more humane, nothing is being done to minimize the anguish.

Nutritional Analysis   *for 1 serving {124 g}*
Calories 105   Calories from fat 31

Nutrient:	% Calories from:	Nutrient:	% Calories from:
Total fat 3 g	29 %	Total carbohydrate 11 g	42 %
Saturated fat 0 g	3 %	Dietary fiber 1 g	
Cholesterol 0 mg		Sugars 0 g	
Sodium 319 mg		Protein 8 g	29 %

% Daily:
Vitamin A, 0 %; Vitamin C, 2 %; Calcium, 4 %; Iron, 6 %

PAT SAJAK
Gin Fizz Egg Pie

8 Servings

3 servings cooking spray (3 seconds of spray)

6 Morningstar* meatless bacon strips

½ teaspoon Heart Beat* canola oil

1 cup chopped onions

3 cups diced tomatoes

1 cup sliced mushrooms

1 package Lightlife Smart Dogs*, cut in 1/4-inch slices

4 ounces shredded Monterey Jack cheese

12 Ener-G* egg substitutes

4 ounces evaporated skim milk

2 ounces Weight Watchers* fat-free Parmesan cheese

8 tablespoons fat-free sour cream

8 pimiento strips

Prepare meatless "bacon" according to manufacturers instructions until just starting to darken. Cool and crumble into small pieces. Preheat oven to 350°F. Coat casserole dish with cooking spray. Sauté onion in oil until beginning to brown. Stir in tomatoes, mushrooms, and "hot dogs"; simmer about 15 minutes. During the last minutes, stir in cheese, reserving 2 tablespoons for the top. Beat egg substitutes until frothy; stir in milk. Combine with pan mixture. Bake 30 minutes; remove from oven and sprinkle Parmesan and reserved Jack cheese over top. Return to oven for 15 minutes, or until pie has a nice golden crust. Allow to cool somewhat before cutting. *Suggestions*: Garnish with thin strips of pimiento and a small dollop of fat-free sour cream.

Nutritional Analysis   *for 1 serving {265 g}*

Calories 179   Calories from fat 27

Nutrient:	% Calories from:	Nutrient:	% Calories from:
Total fat 4 g	17 %	Total carbohydrate 17 g	40 %
Saturated fat 1 g	6 %	Dietary fiber 2 g	
Cholesterol 7 mg		Sugars 3 g	
Sodium 586 mg		Protein 18 g	43 %

% Daily:

Vitamin A, 14 %; Vitamin C, 25 %; Calcium, 20 %; Iron, 143 %   179

WILLARD SCOTT
Baked Rice

4 Servings

*2 servings cooking spray
(2 seconds of spray)*

*1 tablespoon Nucoa Smart
Beat* low-fat margarine*

*1 large onion, peeled and
diced*

1 teaspoon miso

20 ounces water

1 cup uncooked rice

Preheat oven to 350°F. Lightly coat a casserole dish with cooking spray. Lightly coat a skillet with cooking spray and melt margarine. Sauté onion until tender and golden. Dissolve miso in water, and add to onions along with rice. Stir and transfer to casserole dish. Bake covered for 1 hour. Remove from oven and serve directly from casserole dish. *Variation:* Add snipped scallions to rice before baking.

Flax oil has about twice the essential Omega-3 fatty acids as fish. Deficiencies of this "brainfood" may contribute to a variety of conditions such as low energy, skin problems, even a form of diabetes. Omega-3s effectively decrease allergic responses, reduce inflammations, relieve asthma, and slow the production of toxic biochemicals under stress.

Nutritional Analysis *for 1 serving {240 g}*

Calories 196   Calories from fat 14

Nutrient:	% Calories from:	Nutrient:	% Calories from:
Total fat 2 g	8 %	Total carbohydrate 41 g	84 %
Saturated fat 0 g	0 %	Dietary fiber 1 g	
Cholesterol 0 mg		Sugars 4 g	
Sodium 86 mg		Protein 4 g	8 %

% Daily:

Vitamin A, 4 %; Vitamin C, 4 %; Calcium, 3 %; Iron, 12 %

JOAN VAN ARK
Pasta With Pesto Sauce and Broccoli

4 Servings

1 8-ounce stalk broccoli
1 pound fresh pasta
2 garlic cloves, peeled
¾ ounce Ann's* pine nuts
½ teaspoon crushed red pepper
½ teaspoon black pepper
1 tablespoon olive oil
3 tablespoons water
2 ounces grated fat-free Parmesan cheese
½ teaspoon salt

Steam broccoli until barely tender. Drop pasta into boiling water, cook until al dente, and drain. Transfer broccoli to blender or food processor along with Parmesan cheese, garlic, pine nuts, salt and pepper. While machine is running, add olive oil slowly until thoroughly blended. Thin with up to 3 tablespoons water, if too thick. Toss with steaming-hot pasta. *Suggestion:* Use this pesto sauce to make Robin Leach's Cassis Caviar (page 170).

It takes 2,500 gallons of water to produce a pound of beef compared to 25 gallons for a pound of wheat. For every 40 gallons of water a day used to produce a meat-eater's diet, a vegetarian diet uses 3. One acre of land can produce 165 pounds of beef or 20,000 pounds of potatoes.

Nutritional Analysis   *for 1 serving {207 g}*

Calories 287   Calories from fat 67

Nutrient:	% Calories from:	Nutrient:	% Calories from:
Total fat 7 g	26 %	Total carbohydrate 35 g	54 %
Saturated fat 1 g	4 %	Dietary fiber 4 g	
Cholesterol 47 mg		Sugars 1 g	
Sodium 555 mg		Protein 13 g	20 %

% Daily:
Vitamin A, 2 %; Vitamin C, 86 %; Calcium, 4 %; Iron, 10 %

BARBARA WALTERS
Roasted Eggplant Soup

6 Servings

*2 servings cooking spray
(2 seconds of spray)*

1½ tablespoons olive oil

3 tablespoons warm water

*1½ pounds shiny eggplants,
washed and halved*

1 large red onion

1 large red bell pepper

2 medium-size ripe tomatoes

*2 garlic cloves, peeled and
chopped*

*½ teaspoon dried thyme or 4
or 5 branches of fresh thyme*

1 bay leaf

1 teaspoon dried basil

*2 tablespoons fresh basil,
chopped*

*7 cups water (or vegetable
stock)*

1 teaspoon salt

2 tablespoons lemon juice

Preheat oven to 400°F. Lightly coat baking pan with cooking spray. Mix 1 tablespoon of the oil with 3 tablespoons warm water. Brush eggplants, onion, pepper, and tomatoes with oil-water mix, pricking eggplant so oil sinks in. Bake eggplant for 20 minutes, then add onion, pepper, and tomatoes. Cook until eggplant is soft and beginning to collapse, and the skins of all the vegetables are loose, wrinkled, and blackened. Remove from oven, cool briefly, and remove all skins. Seed the pepper and roughly chop all vegetables. Lightly coat bottom of soup pot with cooking spray. Warm remaining olive oil with the garlic and dried herbs. After several minutes add the baked vegetables, salt, and fresh basil. Pour in the water or stock and bring to a boil. Cover and simmer for 25 minutes. Cool the soup briefly, then purée, preserving some texture. Return it to the pot and season to taste with salt and lemon juice. Thin with extra water or stock, as needed.

Nutritional Analysis   *for 1 serving {503 g}*

Calories 97   Calories from fat 37

Nutrient: % Calories from:	Nutrient: % Calories from:
Total fat 4 g 35 %	Total carbohydrate 15 g 57 %
Saturated fat 1 g 4 %	Dietary fiber 1 g
Cholesterol 0 mg	Sugars 3 g
Sodium 374 mg	Protein 2 g 9 %

% Daily:
Vitamin A, 3 %; Vitamin C, 17 %; Calcium, 3 %; Iron, 11 %

DENNIS WEAVER
Dennis and Gerry's Vegetable Soup

6 Servings

1 serving cooking spray (1-second spray)

1 medium onion, chopped

6 celery stalks, chopped

2 carrots, chopped

2 tablespoons Nucoa Smart Beat* low-fat margarine

8 ounces (or more) tomato juice

5 ripe tomatoes, blended (liquefied)

2 cups bottled water

1 small zucchini, chopped

1 cup cooked brown rice

½ cup shredded cabbage

3 sprigs watercress

3 tablespoons La Choy Lite* soy sauce or liquid amino acids

½ teaspoon fines herbes (or to taste)

Coat skillet lightly with cooking spray. Sauté chopped onion, celery, and carrots in margarine until medium cooked, about 10 minutes. Mix in tomato juice, blended tomatoes, and water. Add zucchini, rice, cabbage, watercress, soy sauce, and herbs. Cook until tender—about 5 minutes. Serve immediately.

Nutritional Analysis   *for 1 serving {405 g}*

Calories 119   Calories from fat 20

Nutrient:	% Calories from:	Nutrient:	% Calories from:
Total fat 2 g	16 %	Total carbohydrate 23 g	70 %
Saturated fat 1 g	7 %	Dietary fiber 4 g	
Cholesterol 4 mg		Sugars 8 g	
Sodium 465 mg		Protein 5 g	15 %

% Daily:

Vitamin A, 79 %; Vitamin C, 70 %; Calcium, 9 %; Iron 10 %

VANNA WHITE
Cottage Cheese Salad

6 Servings

32 ounces Knudsen fat-free
cottage cheese*

1 2.5 ounce package Emes
vegetarian gelatin dessert*

*8 ounces crushed pineapple
(packed in juice)*

8 ounces Redi-Wip Lite
topping*

Blend cottage cheese until
smooth. In a bowl mix cottage cheese and your
favorite-flavor vegetarian
gelatin. Drain pineapple
and add to mixture. Fold in
whipped topping. Refrigerate until ready to serve.
Suggestion: Garnish with
fresh whole strawberries.

*Concerned about world
hunger? Twenty pure veg-
etarians can be fed using
the same amount of land
that it takes to feed one
meat-eater. The least
efficient plant food is
about ten times more efficient in terms of energy
returned than the most
efficient animal food.
One-third of all the grain
in the world is fed to animals to produce meat.
Forty thousand children
starve to death every
day. If the American peo-
ple reduced their meat
consumption by a mere
10 percent, sixty million
people could be fed.*

Nutritional Analysis   *for 1 serving {239 g}*

Calories 213   Calories from fat 34

Nutrient: % Calories from:		Nutrient: % Calories from:	
Total fat 4 g	15 %	Total carbohydrate 28 g	49 %
Saturated fat 0 g	0 %	Dietary fiber 2 g	
Cholesterol 7 mg		Sugars 11 g	
Sodium 422 mg		Protein 20 g	36 %

% Daily:

Vitamin A, 0 %; Vitamin C, 6 %; Calcium, 9 %; Iron, 1 %

PART 3

MENU PLANNING

WITH CELEBRITY RECIPES

APPETIZERS

Christmas Pickles · Amy Grant

Hot Artichoke Dip · Tippi Hedren

Marty's Nutty Cheese Roll · Shirley Jones and Marty Ingels

My Brother's Salsa · Joanna Kerns

Cassis Caviar · Robin Leach

Joan's Hummus · Joan Van Ark

DESSERTS & SWEETS

Carrot-Zucchini Muffins · Captain Kangaroo

Aunt Carol's Banana Wanana Nutty Wuddy Bread · Carol Connors

Dot's Bread Pudding · Roger Ebert

Marshmallow Sweet Potatoes · Mickey Gilley

Bob's Favorite Lemon Pie · Bob Hope

Corn Pudding · Will Hutchins

Thomas Jefferson's Chess Pie · Anne Jeffreys

Walnut Trifle · Deborah Kerr

Hilda's Caramel Custard · Geraldo Rivera

Fat-Free Oat Bran Muffins · Daniel J. Travanti

Cottage Cheese Salad · Vanna White

ENTRÉES & CASSEROLES

Nut Loaf · Grant Aleksander

Cajun Red Beans and Rice · Steve Allen and Jayne Meadows

Tim's Favorite Manly Man Lasagne · Tim Allen

Desi and Amy's Pasta Delight · Desi Arnaz Jr.

Mango–Black-Bean Sauce Over Rice · Anne Bancroft and Mel Brooks

Broccoli-Farfel Stuffing · Dyan Cannon

Saffron Risotto With Arugula and Wild Mushrooms · Phoebe Cates

Chevy and Jayni's Vegetable Lasagne · Chevy Chase

Vegetable Cottage Pie · Julie Christie

Sicilian Cheese Casserole · Doris Day

Stuffed and Rolled Eggplant Marinara · Dom DeLuise

Parmesan Eggplant Casserole · Phyllis Diller

Herbed Zucchini Latkes With Roasted Peppers · Julia Duffy

Givetch · Kim Hunter

Fettuccine Alfredo · James Earl Jones

Indonesian Salad With Spicy Peanut Dressing · k. d. Lang

Pasta With Fresh Tomatoes · Hayley Mills

Eggplant Sauce With Pasta · Julie Newmar

Pasta With Tomato Sauce · Tatum O'Neal

Tofu Burgers · Fred Rogers

Gin Fizz Egg Pie · Pat Sajak

GRAINS & LEGUMES

O'Redgrave's Irish Soda Bread · Lynn Redgrave

Estelle's Baked Beans · Carl Reiner

Baked Rice · Willard Scott

HOT VEGGIES

Balsamic Roasted New Potatoes · Ed Asner

Vegetable Medley · Carol Burnett

Hot 'n' Spicy Okra · Joanna Cassidy

Roasted Brussels Sprouts · Marge Champion

Grilled Veggies · Judy Collins

Potatoes Lynda · Lynda Day-George

Steamed Veggies · Anne Francis

SALADS & DRESSINGS

Greek Pasta Salad · Richard Anderson

Tabouli My Way · Paul Anka

Caesar Salad · Lynda Carter

Chicory and Kidney Bean Salad · Tim Conway

Low-Cal Vinaigrette · Elizabeth Taylor

SOUPS & STEWS

Soup Francine · Julie Andrews

Minestrone · Art Linkletter

Ratatouille · Gregory Peck

Vegetable Health Soup · Brooke Shields

Roasted Eggplant Soup · Barbara Walters

Dennis and Gerry's Vegetable Soup · Dennis Weaver

GLOSSARY

agar agar	sea vegetable gelatin; thickening agent used instead of animal gelatin
amino acids	a group of twenty-two organic compounds that underlie protein synthesis, eight of which cannot be manufactured by the body and must be derived from dietary sources
antioxidants	compounds that attack and neutralize free radicals; includes vitamins C, beta-carotene, and certain minerals; these compounds promote healing and slow aging
arrowroot	starchy flour used as a thickening agent; less processed than cornstarch and can be substituted measure for measure
arugula	aromatic, leafy green vegetable with a slightly bitter taste
beetroot	same as beet
bulgur	hulled and partially cooked cracked wheat; quick-cooking grain used for salads, soups, etc.
cellophane noodles	translucent noodles made from mung beans or rice
Chinese cabbage	member of cruciferous family of leafy vegetables
cilantro	Spanish coriander leaves used fresh as an herb
couscous	steamed, dried, and ground durum wheat; used in Middle Eastern cuisine
cracker meal	crushed, sifted, unsweetened crackers used for coating, topping or thickening

dill	an aromatic plant producing pungent leaves and seeds that are used to flavor foods; related to parsley
Egg Replacer: Ener-G	vegan egg substitute used to bind and leaven cooked and baked foods
free radical	toxic oxygen molecule that "rusts" the body, promotes aging, and weakens the immune system: neutralized by antioxidants
garbanzos	chickpeas; light brown beans with a nutty flavor
jicama	root vegetable; taste resembles that of apples or pears
kale	variety of cabbage or greens; use leaves in manner like spinach
lacto-	combining form meaning *milk*
marjoram	aromatic herb of the mint family; related to oregano
mirin	sweet rice cooking wine
miso	thick, salty paste made from fermented soybeans; used for soups and stir-frys
mung beans	small round bean commonly used for bean sprouts
nori	paper-thin sea vegetable; Japan consumes about 9 billion sheets a year
ovo-	combining form meaning *eggs*
pepperoncini	Italian peppers; may be red or green
pesto	a sauce of ground fresh basil, garlic and olive oil usually served over pasta

phyllo	very thin pastry sheets; used to make puff pastry
plantain	a fruit like a banana but larger and with more starch; eaten cooked
quinoa	a whole grain supplying all the essential amino acids in a balanced pattern; highest quality protein of any grain
RDA	recommended daily allowance of vitamins and nutrients determined by the federal government
rice milk	vegan alternative to milk made from rice
risotto	rice prepared by gently sautéing in oil before the addition of water or stock
saffron	aromatic herb used to flavor and color foods
sago	a starch used to thicken puddings
saturated fat	the "bad" fat found in animal foods that clogs arteries
savory	an aromatic plant of the mint family
semivegetarian	one who primarily abstains from eating animal foods
sesame seeds	tasty little seeds usually roasted, toasted, or ground; rich in calcium
shiitake	most popular Japanese mushroom
shoyu	all-purpose Japanese soy sauce
Smart Dogs	brand of meatless franks; 0 cholesterol, 40 calories, 8 g protein
soy milk	liquid pressed from puréed soybeans; nutritionally similar to dairy milk; used to make silken tofu

tahini	smooth, creamy paste made from sesame seeds; 19 percent protein
tamari	kind of soy sauce; similar to shoyu
tapioca	starchy substance obtained by drying the cassava root; used as thickening agent
tarragon	slightly bitter, aromatic herb used in seasoning
tempeh	high-protein cultured food made from soybeans or sometimes from grain
tofu	versatile soybean curd, high in protein, amino acids, vitamins, minerals, and calcium; contains no cholesterol
Tofu Pups	brand of meatless frank; 92 calories, 5.4 g fat per dog
vegan	diet completely free of animal foods
vegetarian	one who abstains from eating animal foods; may use dairy or eggs
vitamins	complex organic substances found in foods and essential for normal metabolic function
wakame	dark green sea vegetable; high in calcium, fiber, antioxidants, and minerals